MONGODB

ON

AWS

Deployment and Administration

Sumit Saraswat

Cover design by

CreateSpace

ISBN: 978-0692506455

First Edition: September 2015

MongoDB on AWS

For my Grandmother

smt. Shantidevi Sharma

Contents

CONTENTS...III

PREFACE..VII

CHAPTER 1..1

NOSQL AND MONGODB...1

    Columnar Databases...2
    Key-Value Databases...2
    Graph Store Databases...3
    Document Store Databases -MongoDB..3

CHAPTER 2..9

CLOUD COMPUTING AND AWS..9

    Cloud computing service models...9
    AWS -commonly used terms..11
    Launching our first EC2 instance..15
    Connecting to Linux Instance using putty..21
    Configure AWS command line interface (CLI)..24
    Terminate the Instance..26

CHAPTER 3..27

MONGODB ON EC2...27

    Manual Deployment..27
    Creating admin user..37
    Sample Collection/Document import...39
    Master Slave replication..42
    Server diagnostics-Quick health check...46
    Data processing using slave instance..48
    Master-slave replication options...49
    What happens when master goes down?..49
    Templated Deployment..52
    Connecting to Instance inside private subnet..58

MongoDB on AWS

Starting Mongod 62

Data directory-Under the hood 63

RAM considerations 66

AWS instance selection 69

You don't need to be right the first time 70

MongoDB operations Log (opLog) 71

Oplog Sizing 72

Oplog sizing imperatives 73

CHAPTER 4 .... **75**

MONGODB CLUSTER-REPLICA SET **75**

MongoDB Replica Set 76

Deployment Scenarios 79

HA in action 90

Priority 0 Replica Set Members 100

Hidden Replica Set Members 108

Delayed Replica Set Members 110

Replica set with arbiter 113

Read semantics 123

Read preference modes 124

Replication backstage tour 126

Replication lag 128

Appropriate Write Concern 130

Elections to select Primary member 131

Replica-set deployment considerations 134

CHAPTER 5 .... **143**

HORIZONTAL SCALING – SHARDING **143**

Sharding components 145

Data distribution and chunk migration 147

Shard key selection 153

Deploying a sharded cluster using MMS 158

Adding a new shard using MMS 169

Location aware sharding 176

IV

Sharding under the hood 182

Sharding deployment considerations 187

CHAPTER 6 .... **193**

MONGODB STORAGE ON AWS ECOSYSTEM **193**

MongoDB space considerations 197

Data Files 197

Journal Files 198

File system snapshots 203

MongoDB storage on AWS 203

Memory mapped storage engine 206

Scaling MongoDB storage on AWS 207

EBS with RAID10 configuration 207

EBS with RAID0 configuration 208

CHAPTER 7 .... **211**

BACKUP AND RESTORE **211**

mongodump and mongorestore 212

EBS Snapshot using EC2 Console 215

EBS Snapshot using AWS CLI 220

Restoring Volume using EC2 Console 222

Restoring Volume using AWS CLI 224

Backups from slave 225

Using MMS for Backup/restore 226

CHAPTER 8 .... **233**

MONITORING **233**

Cluster statistics 233

Database statistics 236

Collection statistics 238

Operation statistics 239

Monitoring using MMS 242

Monitoring using AWS Cloud watch 248

CloudWatch custom metrics (using monitoring scripts) 251

Monitoring alarms. *255*

ADDITIONAL REFERENCES ....**CCLIX**

VI

Preface

Audience

This book is for anyone trying to get started with deploying MongoDB clusters on AWS. This book needs some Linux knowledge and familiarity with general programming concepts.

Omissions

This book does not go into details of mongoDB concepts of Indexing, Aggregation and database performance tuning. The objective of this book is to get audience familiarity with administering and deploying MongoDB clusters on AWS.
Readers may want to skip chapters 2 if they are already acquainted with Amazon Web Services.

Acknowledgements

Author would like to thank the following people
Parents Mrs Kusum Saraswat and Mr D.V. Saraswat for their love and guidance.
Mrs and Mr H.M. Saraswat for their encouragement and support.
Surbhi and Peeyush Tugnawat for providing moral support.
Sandeep Shekhawat, Yashu Vyas and Abhishek Sinha for technical feedback.
Mira and Mishti for being guardian angels they are , and last but not the least his better half Shweta Saraswat for supporting him throughout this journey.

MongoDB on AWS

VIII

Chapter 1

NoSQL and MongoDB

A NoSQL (originally referring to "non SQL") database provides a mechanism for storage and retrieval of data that is modeled in means other than the tabular relations used in traditional relational databases.

-Wikipedia

L ong before the advent of web, data was visualized in terms of structured schema. With the arrival of web and whole gambit of web enabled devices came the stock pile of schema less data. Think of weblogs or clickstream data they follow no set schema. Other than storing the whole file in a single field (wherein all the granular information that can be analyzed is lost) , there are limited options when considering relational schema environment.

NoSQL was a step forward to break this ceiling of retrofitting everything into traditional schema design. The idea was to retrofit the schema to suit the data. *NoSQL* stands for *"Not only SQL"* to signify the fact that NoSQL databases can do what a SQL database can and much more than a traditional database can never do. The motivation behind NoSQL is simplified design, scalable and high availability architecture.

No SQL world can be broadly categorized into 4 different database types

Columnar Databases

Columnar databases or Column store databases store data in columns space. All columns are treated individually and values of columns are stored column store databases are stored together. They are well suited for OLAP and aggregate queries. Columnar storage is perfect for systems where all values (or most values) of column are analyzed together most often. Columnar data allows escape from full table scans that happen in a row oriented DBMS, although only certain columns are needed for analysis.

Column storage of data also allows for a high degree of compression, which in turn allows for reduced CPU/memory usage and low disk I/O. Column storage also allows for easy index builds on columns.

Key-Value Databases

Key-value databases still store data unstructured records, but there is a method to the madness. Key value database store header information for a field , but not as a separate record like traditional database. The header information for the record is provided as a key and value associated with it stores the actual column value.

Unlike a traditional RDBMS a key has no defined nature it can be anything ay format , of any length, its sole existence is to provide information about the value it stores.

Storing data as key value pairs makes them super flexible for reading and writing data based on a key. Key value databases are widely used in embedded systems or as in process databases.

Redis,DynamoDB and *Riak* are some examples of Key-value databases

Graph Store Databases

Graph databases are designed based on graph theory they make extensive use of Graphical elements like nodes, properties and edges. Nodes represent traceable entities such as people or businesses.Properties are relevant information that relate to nodes .Edges are the lines that connect nodes to nodes or nodes to properties and they represent the relationship between the two.

Elements in graph databases are interjoined with an many-to-many relations between them.

Document Store Databases -MongoDB

In a document-oriented approach to storing data, data is stored as a document, and documents are clubbed together as collections. Documents in the collection are identified by a unique key.

MongoDB is a type of document store database. *MongoDB* places all its related data together, data can be spread across multiple servers and each server is responsible for its own dataset.

MongoDB scales horizontally by sacrificing transactional support (this is true for almost all NoSQL environments),Out of Consistency, Partitioning and availability at least one parameter will not be guaranteed.

There is no concept of fixed schema in *MongoDB* also absent is a concept like unique constraint (there is a unique index though) or Mass-Update. Unlike traditional RDBMS MongoDB does not provide JOIN functionality, instead all the related data is stored in a single "place" (or appropriately in a single document).

MongoDB makes use of server RAM to spool the data during reads, the data set and indexes residing on the RAM are known as working set. If *MongoDB* does not find data on the RAM during read operations it will load the page from disk to memory, if memory is not enough it will swap the data from working set with the page it needs inside RAM. To support large datasets and avoid this kind of paging to the disk *MongoDB* divides the datasets across servers known as shards (more on shard in *Chapter 5*). Sharding is important concept and it's important to understand it for performance imperatives.

A typical production deployment will have multiple databases, each database is made up of collections (akin to tables in RDBMS) and each collection comprises of documents (similar to rows in a RDBMS table).

RDBMS terminology	MongoDB equivalent
Tables	Collection
Rows/Records	Documents
Partition	Shard
Partition key	Shard Key

MongoDB uses Binary JSON to store documents, in other words MongoDB stores JSON document in binary encoded format. Documents in MongoDB are stored in key value pair, thus providing the schema-less flexibility MongoDB is famous for.

It's worth looking at how MongoDB handles data consistency, hardware scaling and data availability.

Availability

MongoDB uses master slave setup to increase availability of data in the cluster. Using a master slave setup (termed replica sets) data redundancy is achieved to make data available from more than one source. During replication data is propagated to multiple nodes and the clients can get to the data even when the primary node is down. In a replica set all write requests go to the master node (primary) , data is subsequently written to slave nodes (secondaries).

Replica sets also allow *MongoDB* to achieve automatic failover. In case of primary node going down cluster chooses a new master among them and application start writing to the new master. All this happens seamlessly and without the knowledge of client applications. Elections can be rigged to favor certain nodes to become master (Nodes that may have better memory and CPU).

Scalability

MongoDB allows and supports horizontal scaling. The way *MongoDB* replica sets are designed allows for scaling the cluster for both read and write scaling. we can add slave nodes to cater to read requests from client applications thus diverting some of the read traffic hitting the primary nodes. We can also partition the data by using a concept known as shards to keep the logically related data clubbed together for better fetch to miss ratio.

Performance

MongoDB supports data indexing, that allows faster queries. *MongoDB* is designed with schema that supports embedded documents and arrays, this negates the need for joins that consumes most CPU and other memory resources in a traditional RDBMS.

Consistency

MongoDB achieves data consistency by using a cluster of machines running in replica sets. It also has inherent mechanism to wait for the writes to be replicated to all or configured number of slaves. The level of consistency can be engineered on mongoDB to specify number of servers the write needs to go before termed a success. Replica sets give the flexibility of reading data from slaves thus reducing bottlenecks on the master nodes and increasing the read performance.

Chapter 2

Cloud computing and AWS

AWS is growing at the rate of 49 percent YOY. AWS revenue reached $6.2 Billion in revenue and is targeted to reach $6.2 Billion in 2015.

Amazon financial earning report (Q2 2015)

Cloud computing makes it easy to access and store your data and computing resources via internet. In layman's term cloud computing is a relocating your hard ware and software from your home into internet , making it available from anywhere. Actual technicalities involved in cloud computing go little farther than simply storing and accessing information.

Cloud computing service models

Infrastructure as a Service (IaaS) :Infrastructure as a service is a synonym for providing hardware, servers, and networking components on the internet. The consumer (i.e. we) don't have to worry about buying and upkeep of costly servers, the provider (i.e. Amazon/Google or microsoft) is responsible for running and maintaining the server. Speaking specifically of AWS, Amazon also provides user interface and APIs for configuration and customization of these servers on demand. So if you are company of 1 or 100 people you have the choice of procuring similar hardware, and pay what you use.

Platform as a Service (PaaS): In platform as a service , hardware and software tools are provided in a subscription model. To develop an application you need certain computing resources, *PaaS* provides Consumers with readymade access to operating system, programming environment, database, etc. to develop their apps . A provider for *PasS* hosts all these infrastructure pieces on their environment freeing the users to devout man-hours on the actual development of their applications.

Force.com from salesforce is an example of PaaS, similarly *ElasticBeanStalk* provided by AWS falls in the category of *PasS*.

Software as a Service (SaaS): As the name suggest SaaS is metaphor for providing pre-installed software on a subscribed "on-demand" basis. Amazon customers can buy the subscription via AWS marketplace. Users can buy and configure operating system images of pre-installed databases, web applications, and BI software etc. Most application users know how to use the software but not necessarily accustomed with the nuances of installing them. Some users may want to use all their man hours developing rather than troubleshooting and optimizing installation issues, *SaaS* model is appropriate for them.

Cloud computing and AWS

So what kind of service does AWS provides? AWS provides all these models under the same umbrella , saving you the heartache of co-coordinating with separate vendors to virtualize your environment on cloud. Apart from ease of getting everything under one roof , customers don't have to spend time in making all these virtual environments talk to each other.

AWS -commonly used terms

Let's quickly cruise through some key terms that we will be seeing a lot during this book ,they will be revealed in detail at appropriate sections in subsequent chapters. Treat this as a primer to get us quickly acclimatized with common AWS terminology.

Regions and Availability zones

Amazon is a global company and to has data centers around the globe for reasons of server locality. Amazon provides AWS products and services by categorizing them under different regions.

There are multiple reasons for that , connecting to region closest to you provides the lowest latency , and also fulfills legal obligation in case you are required to keep the data in your specific geography (as is the case in some European companies). keeping regions separate also allows amazon to device independent pricing for services it offers. Regions are isolated from each other, any communication across regions happen across wan. The network latency while communicating between regions will vary based on the ping distance.

A region is further subdivided into availability zones. The way Availability Zone(s) are designed is to make each availability zone (AZ) as a separate entity but connected to other availability zones via low latency network. This way we get the best of both, isolate the availability zone(AZ) from what's happening in other AZ's yet have low latency communication between AZ's.

For example North America that has 4 regions, and multiple availability zones under each region.

US East (Northern Virginia) Region EC2 Availability Zones: 5
US West (Northern California) Region EC2 Availability Zones: 3
US West (Oregon) Region EC2 Availability Zones: 3
AWS GovCloud (US) Region

> EC2 Availability Zones: 2

EC2 Instances

EC2 stands for Amazon Elastic Compute Cloud, this is what we will be designating as our mongoDB servers in subsequent chapters. EC2 is a virtual machine launched using the servers in Amazon's data center. When we launch the EC2 instance we can configure the capacity and other hardware characteristics we need, these hardware parameters are not set in stone and are easily reconfigurable.

Subnets and VPC

AWS provides the freedom of setting up a virtual data center inside cloud .this way you can configure your own security and access parameters just like a traditional data center. This dedicated piece of cloud us known as virtual private cloud (VPC), it's a virtual network configured for a specific AWS account. Every VPC is logically isolated from other VPC's and is easily scalable. If you don't specify a VPC all instances are launched in a default VPC.

When you launch your instances inside a Virtual network (VPC) , you may want to segment your traffic based on your security and operational needs .A subnet allows you to do that so you may have a private subnet that lies inside of firewall with no access from internet and a public subnet(with possibly a NAT server) that will interface with internet traffic.

Each instance that you launch has at least one security group attached to it, security group allows you to configure and control inbound and outbound traffic. You can always attach more than one security group when you launch your instance.

EBS backed Volume

EBS stands for elastic block store, and provides block level storage for AWS EC2 instances. In an on premise server raw storage volumes are created and mounted on server directories for OS to use them as individual drives, similarly we mount an Amazon EBS volume to an EC2 instance. For obvious reasons each volume can be attached to only one EC2 instance, but we can attach multiple Amazon EBS volumes to an EC2 instance. An EBS volume is reusable and can be easily detached from one EC2 instance and attached to another (just like a physical hard drive).

EBS volumes can be further classified into Standard and Provisioned IOPS volumes. You may need IOPS EBS volumes for OLTP type of workloads where you need consistent IO performance, for general cases standard EBS volume suffice.

An EBS volume allows backing up the data by creating snapshots. These snapshots are stored in amazons inexpensive online storage system called Amazon S3. We can use the EBS snapshot to create EBS volume and attach it to an EC2 instance if needed.

Cloud formation Templates

EC2 provisioning in AWS is straightforward and as easy as point and click using the GUI . If you are provisioning resources that have specific parameters and you are doing that multiple times, AWS provides a template that can be reused for every such iteration. The templates are known as CloudFormation templates and enable you to provision the same AWS resources repeatedly.

We will talk about cloud formation during replica sets,we will deploy EC2 instances using cloud formation templates during replica set deployments.

Let's launch one EC2 instance to experience how easy it is to procure an EC2 resource.

Launching our first EC2 instance

Note : If you are doing this for the first time , you may be eligible for the free tier (depending on whether it's still being offered by Amazon) . If you are not being offered free tier you will be charged for launching the instance.

1. Open the Amazon EC2 console
   at *https://console.aws.amazon.com/ec2/.*

2. From the console dashboard, click Launch Instance.

3. The next page will give you a choice of Amazon machine instance (AMI).AMI is a template containing OS and hardware configuration. Choose Amazon Linux AMI for this exercise.

4. The next page will give a list of EC2 product families, with hardware configuration for each instance. for this particular iteration we will choose *t2.micro*.

5. Under "3. *configure instance*" , we will need to select a VPC if you don't select a VPC default VPC will be selected for you .

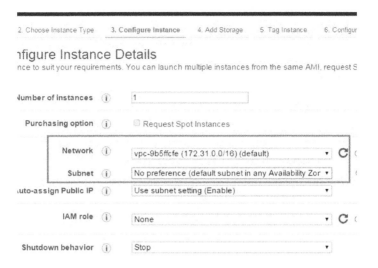

6. While still under *"3. configure instance"*, for the subnet choose *No Preference* and the instance will be launched in any availability zone you are in.

7. Under *"6. Configure Security group"*, select the radio button for *"Create a new security group"*.

8. Go to *"7. Review"* and click on Launch.we will get two drop down menus/ in the top menu select "create a new key pair.

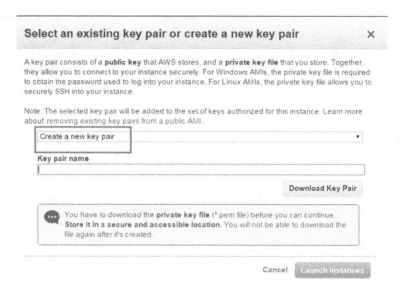

9. Enter a name for the key pair, and then click *"Download Key Pair"*, save the private key file in your local desktop.

10. A file with **.pem** extension will be generated and saved at the location we specified in the previous step.

    We will get a *.ppk* file for this *.pem* file, to convert or get to the *.ppk* file for this *.pem* file do the following

    o Download puttygen from

      http:// www.chiark.greenend.org.uk/ ~ sgtatham/ putty/ download.html

    o Open puttygen, Select the SSH-2 RSA option and click on the Load button.

o In the file, select the .pem file that we saved in local desktop

o   We should see successfully imported private file after the
.pem file is imported

o click on the Save private key option and save the file with any name. The file will have a .ppk suffix

11. click Launch Instances,A confirmation comes up stating *"your instances are now launching"*. Click on *"View Instances"* button on bottom right of the confirmation page.

12. The next screen should show instance id , instance state etc and a public DNS for the instance just launched. We will connect to our instance using this public DNS

Connecting to Linux Instance using putty

1. Open PuTTY , in the host name give the public DNS

2. Under ssh →auth , browse for the .ppk file we generated in the previous section

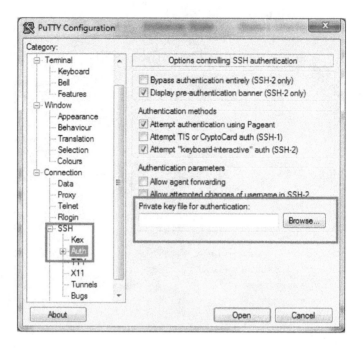

Use Port 22 and connection type as ssh

3. Once the session starts, In the login as, use "ec2-user" as the login user name.

   Every time we launch this instance we will be required to provide the private key. If you don't want to give users connecting to the instance to every time provide this key during connect, we can configure SSH with passwords instead.

   o Create a new user in EC2 (use *https://console.aws.amazon.com/iam/* to create new user and assign permissions to this user),Also allow the new

user to have sudo su privilges by editing
/etc/sudoers.d/cloud-init

- o Using vi editor open the file */etc/ssh/sshd_config*
- o Comment out the following two entries (take out the # in front of the entry)

```
PasswordAuthentication yes

ChallengeResponseAuthentication yes
```

Save and close */etc/ssh/sshd_config*

- o After taking the backup of authorized key files placed at *rm -f /home/ec2-user/.ssh/* and *rm -f /root/.ssh/* remove these files

```
rm -f /home/ec2-user/.ssh/authorized_keys

rm -f /root/.ssh/authorized_keys
```

- o Restart sshd

```
$ sudo service sshd restart
Stopping sshd:                          [ OK ]
Starting sshd:                          [ OK ]
```

Note: Using password authentication alone leaves lot of security loopholes specially for root user. It's recommended to use multifactor authentication (MFA) for EC2 instances, MFA introduces an extra layer of security adding a AWS MFA device authentication code.[1]

Configure AWS command line interface (CLI)

AWS CLI comes preinstalled on amazon EC2 instances , the CLI needs to be configured for the specific user account using simple configuration steps.

1. Execute *"aws configure"* command and provide the access key and access key id for your account, enter the default region name where the instance is launched.

```
$ aws configure
AWS Access Key ID [None]: AKIAIHSS3Q4YJ62CMY2Q
AWS Secret Access Key [None]: euFqZjn0SSJ4RwKniAuP6axtASSUZc3uyn
Default region name [None]: us-east-1
Default output format [None]: json:
```

Go to home directory for the account user by executing cd ~,.*aws*

---

[1] Refer AWS IAM documentation at *http://aws.amazon.com/iam/details/mfa/* for more information on enabling multifactor authentication

directory will be visible in the home directory .This is where config files for AWS CLI are stored.

2. The options we gave during "aws config" execution in the previous step are stored in two seperate files under *.aws* directory. If we open file named *'config'* following entries will be visible

```
[default]
output = json
region = us-east-1

~
```

3. In credentials file, we can view the access key id and access key.

```
[default]
AWS Access Key ID : AKIAIHSS3Q4YJ62CMY2Q
AWS Secret Access Key : euFqZjn0SSJ4RwKniAuP6axtASSUZc3uyn

~
```

4. Validate AWS CLI is working for us by executing "aws ec2 describe-instances"

We can use AWS CLI for command line execution of whatever we will be doing in AWS console GUI.we will be using CLI option to take

EBS volume backups (snapshots) and volume restores.

For all the EC2 instances we will be provision in subsequent chapter, execute the configuration steps.

We are done with the exercise to introduce ourselves with prerequisites and steps to provision the EC2 instances.

let's terminate our sample instance.

Terminate the Instance

1. In the AWS EC2 console , select your instance
2. In the action menu , select *Instance State →Terminate*

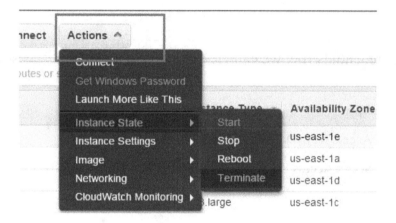

3. Click on "Yes Terminate ", this will shut down the instance that we launched as part of this exercise.

Chapter 3

MongoDB on EC2

Chapter Objectives

➤ *Manually deploy a standalone mongoDB server on EC2 instance*

➤ *Use case for mongoimport utility*

➤ *Deploy a master slave replication using EC2 instances*

➤ *Deploy mongoDB using cloud formation template*

➤ *EC2 selection criteria for mongoDB deployments*

➤ *Operation log and size imperatives*

....

L ets launch a AWS EC2 instance to configure our standalone *MongoDB* server.

Manual Deployment

sign in to AWS management console using your credentials.

http://aws.amazon.com/

Click on EC2 to create a Linux instance for *MongoDB* deployment

1. From the available EC2 instance choice select amazon linux

MongoDB on AWS

2. We will be provided with choice of instances from multiple EC2 family groups. Choose general purpose m4.large for the time being .Each instance family brings unique offerings to the table , we will talk about what instance families are more suitable for *MongoDB*.

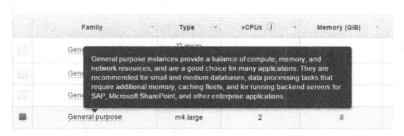

3. From the configure instance tab choose the subnet that lies in the availability zone nearest to you

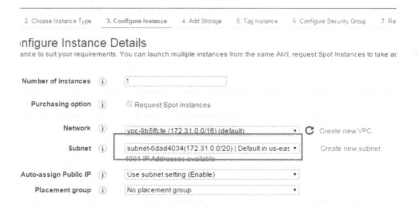

4. In the *add storage* tab add a volume for data directory, make the volume type *Provisioned IOPS* and add the appropriate space for the data you would be hosting for your MongoDB databases.

5. Add two more volumes , we will need separate volumes for */journal* and */log* . **Why separate volumes?** *log* and *Journal* directory contents have different data retention, space and backup requirements than *data* directory. Keeping the volumes separate will allow us to handle these volumes separate from each other.

6. In the security group use a new one or a existing security group that allows for ssh traffic, review your selection
7. Select the key pair for your instance and launch your instance.

8. Log into to AWS console ,You should see instance getting initialized

9. Log into the instance using putty (or any other client tool you prefer)[2]

10. You will enter the instance with ec2-user credentials , to edit any files requiring root permissions do a *sudo* as root user.

11. ***Configuring the package management system:*** Create a file */etc/yum.repos.d/mongodb-org-3.0.repo*

```
sudo view /etc/yum.repos.d/mongodb-org-3.0.repo
```

12. Create an entry in the */etc/yum.repos.d/mongodb-org-3.0.repo*

```
[mongodb-org-3.0]
name=MongoDB Repository
```

---

[2] Refer
http://docs.aws.amazon.com/AWSEC2/latest/UserGuide/AccessingInstances.html for more information if you are using some other tool

```
baseurl=http://repo.mongodb.org/yum/amazon/2013.03/mongodb-
org/3.0/x86_64/

gpgcheck=0

enabled=1
```

13. ***Installing MongoDB package:*** To install *MongoDB* , execute the following command

   sudo yum install -y mongodb-org

   You should see the following message indicating a successful install.

```
Installed:
  mongodb-org.x86_64 0:3.0.3-1.amzn1
Dependency Installed:
  mongodb-org-mongos.x86_64 0:3.0.3-1.amzn1        mongodb-org-
server.x86_64 0:3.0.3-1.amzn1        mongodb-org-shell.x86_64 0:3.0.3-
1.amzn1        mongodb-org-tools.x86_64 0:3.0.3-1.amzn1
Complete!
```

14. Next we will create three directories for data log and journal files

```
# sudo mkdir /data /log /journal
```

15. New volumes were added to our instance, we need to create file systems on the newly added volumes.

sudo mkfs.ext4 /dev/sdb

sudo mkfs.ext4 /dev/sdc

sudo mkfs.ext4 /dev/sdd

```
[root@ip-xxx-xx-xx-xxx /]# sudo mkfs.ext4 /dev/sdb

mke2fs 1.42.12 (29-Aug-2014)

Creating filesystem with 26214400 4k blocks and 6553600 inodes

Filesystem UUID: 95838c95-9658-4ff7-b7f6-cdb49d8d9943

Superblock backups stored on blocks:

     32768, 98304, 163840, 229376, 294912, 819200, 884736,
1605632, 2654208,

     4096000, 7962624, 11239424, 20480000, 23887872


Allocating group tables: done

Writing inode tables: done

Creating journal (32768 blocks): done

Writing superblocks and filesystem accounting information: done

[root@ip-xxx-xx-xx-xxx /]# sudo mkfs.ext4 /dev/sdc

mke2fs 1.42.12 (29-Aug-2014)

Creating filesystem with 10485760 4k blocks and 2621440 inodes
```

Filesystem UUID: 67ada5de-7ffb-463d-ac4c-b2f04e4f04ec

Superblock backups stored on blocks:

    32768, 98304, 163840, 229376, 294912, 819200, 884736, 1605632, 2654208,

    4096000, 7962624

Allocating group tables: done

Writing inode tables: done

Creating journal (32768 blocks): done

Writing superblocks and filesystem accounting information: done

[root@ip-xxx-xx-xx-xxx /]# sudo mkfs.ext4 /dev/sdd

mke2fs 1.42.12 (29-Aug-2014)

Creating filesystem with 10485760 4k blocks and 2621440 inodes

Filesystem UUID: 51348aed-b11e-47be-ba43-2cf75f253406

Superblock backups stored on blocks:

    32768, 98304, 163840, 229376, 294912, 819200, 884736, 1605632, 2654208,

    4096000, 7962624

Allocating group tables: done

Writing inode tables: done

Creating journal (32768 blocks): done

Writing superblocks and filesystem accounting information: done

Note: Use XFS or Ext4 file systems for MongoDB. These file systems have some inherent tuning options suitable for mongoDB. XFS and EXT4 support I/O suspend and write-cache flushing that helps in multi-disk consistent snapshots.

16. We need to create entries about these volumes in file system table , adding the entries in the */etc/fstab* will enable the Linux system to include these mappings between mount point and file system during system boot.

```
/dev/sdb /data ext4 defaults,auto,noatime,noexec 0 0

/dev/sdc /journal ext4 defaults,auto,noatime,noexec 0 0

/dev/sdd /log ext4 defaults,auto,noatime,noexec 0 0
```

17. Mount each of the file systems to the three directories we created, the mount command uses the mapping between mount point and filesystem from */etc/fstab* table.

```
[root@ip-xxx-xx-xx-xxx /]# sudo mount /data

[root@ip-xxx-xx-xx-xxx /]# sudo mount /log

[root@ip-xxx-xx-xx-xxx /]# sudo mount /journal
```

18. ***Change the directory ownership:***Change user and group ownership of newly created directories for *data , log* and *journal* to *mongod*

```
sudo chown mongod:mongod /data /journal /log
```

19. ***Edit the MongoDB configuration file:***We will modify the */etc/mongod.conf* configuration file contents , the new entry in *dbpath* will ensure to let mongod use */data* as the new data directory (comment or remove the exiting entry *dbpath=/var/lib/mongo*)

20. Check the system *ulimit* settings and make sure they are in sync with recommended setting for *MongoDB.*

```
            -f (file size): unlimited

            -t (cpu time): unlimited

            -v (virtual memory): unlimited [1]

            -n (open files): 64000

            -m (memory size): unlimited [1] [2]

            -u (processes/threads): 64000
```

Also make sure that *read-ahead* settings for the block devices that store the database files are appropriate. For random access use patterns, set low *read-ahead* values. A *read-ahead* of 32 (16kb) often works well.

Run *sudo blockdev --report* to check the read-ahead values.

If not appropriate as per standards , change it using the following command in the startup script

sudo blockdev --setra 32 /dev/xvdb

The system resets the *read-ahead* values to default when it reboots,keep it in the startup script to avoid manually setting it everytime.

21. ***Setting the data directory :*** Open */etc/mongod.conf* file and dbpath entry to */data*

22. We are all set , kickstart the mongod daemon

```
[root@ip-xxx-xx-xx-xxx ~]# sudo service mongod start
Starting mongod:                        [OK]
```

23. Check the contents of log file

at */var/log/mongodb/mongod.log*

The text *"waiting for connections on port 27017 "* points to the fact that mongod is running

```
2015-06-13T18:44:52.535+0000 I STORAGE  [FileAllocator] creating
directory /data/_tmp
```

```
2015-06-13T18:44:52.538+0000 I STORAGE  [FileAllocator] done
allocating datafile /data/local.0, size: 64MB,  took 0.001 secs
2015-06-13T18:44:52.544+0000 I NETWORK  [initandlisten] waiting for
connections on port 27017 ~
```

24. Check the status of *MongoDB* services by executing the following command

    ps -ef | grep mongo

```
$ ps -ef | grep mongo
mongod    2556    1 0 18:01 ?      00:00:00 /usr/bin/mongod -f
/etc/mongod.conf
ec2-user  2577  2455  0 18:03 pts/0   00:00:00 grep mongo
```

Creating admin user

We can use the steps mentioned in this section to create new users for *MongoDB* applications.

1. Connect to mongo shell by navigating to */usr/bin/* and then executing the command

   ./mongo

```
# ./mongo
```

```
MongoDB shell version: 3.0.3

connecting to: test

Server has startup warnings:

2015-06-08T12:03:04.637+0000 I CONTROL  [initandlisten]

2015-06-08T12:03:04.637+0000 I CONTROL  [initandlisten] **
WARNING: /sys/kernel/mm/transparent_hugepage/defrag is 'always'.
```

2. We are in mongo shell now, lets create a new admin user while we are at it.

3. To perform any database admin functions we will have to log into admin database. Connect to admin database by executing the *db.getSiblingDB* command

```
> db=db.getSiblingDB('admin')
Admin
```

4. We will add a new user dbadmin with *userAdminAnyDatabase* role

```
> db.createUser(
{
    user: "dbadmin",
```

```
        pwd: "admin",

        roles: [ { role: "userAdminAnyDatabase", db: "admin" } ]

    }

)

Successfully added user: {

    "user" : "dbadmin",

    "roles" : [

        {

                "role" : "userAdminAnyDatabase",

                "db" : "admin"

        }

    ]

}
```

5. Open another shell to test the new *dbadmin* user and execute use *dbadmin* to switch the mongo shell to use *dbadmin* user

```
> use dbadmin

switched to db dbadmin
```

Sample Collection/Document import

In this section we will try to import some data using *mongoimport* utility that comes with standard install of *MongoDB*.

We will import the sample zip codes collection placed at the following *media.mongodb.org* url.

---

http://media.mongodb.org/zips.json?_ga=1.88619867.1932956186.
1433008705

---

mongoimport utility enables bulk imports to MongoDB databases.by default *mongoimport* imports data to localhost using default port 27017.

Note: We can import to any instance reachable from the current EC2 instance by using –h option for a different hostname.

1. ***Download the file from internet:*** Download the file into /zip directory in *MongoDB* server instance

---

```
# wget media.mongodb.org/zips.json

--2015-06-08 17:27:06-- http://media.mongodb.org/zips.json

Resolving media.mongodb.org (media.mongodb.org)... 54.192.102.153,
54.192.102.175, 54.192.102.190, ...

Connecting to media.mongodb.org
(media.mongodb.org)|54.192.102.153|:80... connected.

HTTP request sent, awaiting response... 200 OK
```

```
Length: 3182409 (3.0M) [application/json]

Saving to: 'zips.json'

zips.json                        100%[===================>]

3.03M  --.-KB/s   in 0.05s

2015-06-08 17:27:06 (56.0 MB/s) - 'zips.json' saved [3182409/3182409]
```

2. ***Create a Database:*** Create a new database to host the zip collection, creation of database in *MongoDB* is simple .we will christen the new database as *censusdb*

```
> use censusdb

switched to db censusdb
```

3. ***Importing file to MongoDB database:*** Start one more putty session and execute the import command outside of mongo shell to ingest this file in zip collection inside *censusdb* database

   mongoimport --db censusdb --collection zips --file /zip/zips.json

```
# mongoimport --db censusdb --collection zips --file /zip/zips.json

2015-06-08T17:32:52.255+0000   connected to: localhost

2015-06-08T17:32:53.292+0000   imported 29353 documents
```

4. Query zips collection to make sure data is imported as desired. *show collection* lists all collections in the database and *db.zips.count()* gives the total documents in the collection.

```
> show collections
system.indexes
zips
> db.zips.count()
29353
```

Master Slave replication

Master slave replication is the simplest architecture for maintaining redundancy in *MongoDB*. Master slave replication is simply two running mongod instances: one in master mode, and the other in slave mode.

When we start the mongod in master mode, simply specify the --master option, the mongod will create a *local.oplog.$main* collection, This collection servers as the "operation log" that queues all the operations happening at the master node. The slave node will replicate all these operations from the master into its own data directory.

1. Stop the mongod in the existing instance

```
#sudo service mongod stop
```

2. ***Create a master mongod:*** Start mongod as a master

```
#mongod --master --dbpath /data --fork --logpath /log/mongpdb.log
```

3. ***Creating a new Instance for Slave:*** Start another instance that will work as slave, current instance is running in region *us-east-1e* . The new instance will be launched in a different zone (in the same region)

Go to AWS console , in the actions dropdown choose *"Launch More Like This"*

In the configure instance , choose a subnet in a different availability zone (we don't want both the instances to be unreachable if the zone hosting them becomes unavailable)

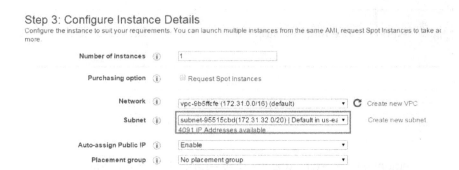

Step 3: Configure Instance Details
Configure the instance to suit your requirements. You can launch multiple instances from the same AMI, request Spot Instances to take a[...] more.

4. Add two volumes for /data and /log respectively

Type		Device	Snapshot	Size (GiB)	Volume Type		IOPS
Root		/dev/xvda	snap-b772aec8	8	General Purpose (SSD)	▼	24 / 3000
EBS	▼	/dev/sde ▼	Search (case-insensitive)	100	General Purpose (SSD)	▼	300 / 3000
EBS	▼	/dev/sdf ▼	Search (case-insensitive)	40	General Purpose (SSD)	▼	120 / 3000

Add New Volume

5. ***Starting mongod as slave:*** Complete the *MongoDB* installation like the master instance, and start the *mongod* as slave

   To start a mongod instance in slave mode, mongod is invoked with *--slave* option

> mongod --slave --source ip-172-31-63-100:27017 --dbpath /data --fork --logpath /log/mongodb.log

6. To view master slave replication in action , we can look at the ***operations log*** (*oplog*) for both master and slave instances. Oplog is a special collection that records the chronological order of operations (read/write etc) that arrive at the master *MongoDB*

instance.The slaves in turn keep a copy of oplog and replicate the similar data changes to its copy of master data.

Observing master oplog: We can Check *oplog* details on master instance using *rs.printReplicationInfo()*

```
> rs.printReplicationInfo()

configured oplog size:   4769.484344482422MB

log length start to end: 1614secs (0.45hrs)

oplog first event time:  Thu Jun 18 2015 00:20:17 GMT+0000 (UTC)

oplog last event time:   Thu Jun 18 2015 00:47:11 GMT+0000 (UTC)

now:                     Thu Jun 18 2015 00:47:20 GMT+0000 (UTC)
```

Observing slave oplog: Similarly on the slave instance, details of the slave oplog can be viewed by using *rs.printSlaveReplicationInfo()* method.

```
> rs.printSlaveReplicationInfo()

source: ip-172-31-63-100:27017

        syncedTo: Thu Jun 18 2015 00:48:11 GMT+0000 (UTC)

    11 secs (0 hrs) behind the freshest member
```

This shows our slave node is replicating from master node with the delay of 11 secs.

Server diagnostics-Quick health check

To do a health check of any server instance use server status command *db.runCommand({"serverStatus":1})*

```
> db.runCommand({"serverStatus":1})
{

      "host" : "ip-172-31-63-100",

      "version" : "3.0.4",

      "process" : "mongod",

      "pid" : NumberLong(3335),

      "uptime" : 1913,

      "uptimeMillis" : NumberLong(1912912),

      "uptimeEstimate" : 1889,

      "localTime" : ISODate("2015-06-18T00:52:10.686Z"),

      "asserts" : {

            "regular" : 0,

            "warning" : 0,

            "msg" : 0,

            "user" : 0,

            "rollovers" : 0

      },
```

```
"backgroundFlushing" : {

        "flushes" : 31,

        "total_ms" : 23,

        "average_ms" : 0.7419354838709677,

        "last_ms" : 2,

        "last_finished" : ISODate("2015-06-18T00:51:17.821Z")

},

"connections" : {

        "current" : 2,

        "available" : 817,

        "totalCreated" : NumberLong(7)

}
```

ServerStatus provides useful information about health of a *MongoDB* server.

Connection provides information on number of connection from client applications.

Available is the number of connections from connection pool available for other client applications.

mem provides statistics on how much data server has memory mapped.

Indexcounter provides information on usage of indexes in mongoDB.

The *accesses filed* represent number of times operations have accessed indexes.

hits represent number of times mongod was able to return the index from memory.

Misses reflect frequency of operations accessing the index outside of memory.

A higher value of *misses* compared to *hits* (also captured in *missRatio*)means you need to upgrade your instance to something that has bigger RAM.

backgroundFlushing provides statistics on mongod flushes from memory to disk. If you want to do a health check on your write performance look at these values closely if write performance is bothering you.

opcounters provide information on operation type for each operation

Data processing using slave instance

Apart from building data redundancy Master slave replication can also be used to offload read traffic from master to slave instances.

When a slave is started, start it with both - -*master* and - - *slave* options. The slave started in master mode can facilitate any write operations to slave apart from replicating data from master. Only caveat when using this mode is never to write to the same database that's being replicated from master, otherwise slave will not know what copy of the operation to keep as golden copy.

Master-slave replication options

--Slavedelay: option to relay oplog contents with customized delay. You may want to do this to make sure information from master flows with some time lag to allow recovery in case database at master is inadvertently deleted or some bad inserts happen.with delayed replication there is a window of opportunity to fix things without affecting all the dependent slaves.

--only: Specify this option if selected databases need to be replicated, the default behavior is to replicate all databases.this option is useful if you are using any slaves for data processing. Do not replicate databases that are being hit with write operations on slave.

What happens when master goes down?

Let's assume the region hosting master instance has power outage or a natural disaster and master instance is unavailable, to simulate this scenario let's stop the master instance manually using the AWS console.

If you execute *rs.printSlaveReplicationInfo()* again on the slave instance , you will find the slave is waiting to be synced with master and is rapidly falling behind the master instance.

```
> rs.printSlaveReplicationInfo()

source: ip-172-31-63-100:27017

        syncedTo: Thu Jun 18 2015 01:01:42 GMT+0000 (UTC)

        101 secs (0.03 hrs) behind the freshest member.
```

Note: When we started the slave it was only 11 secs behind. its farther behind now, after master becomes unavailable.

There is no automatic failover from master to slave, you will have to do a resync of *oplog* once master is up again or worst case scenarios start it as a master and submit all write operations that this erstwhile slave instance might be missing before master went down.

Master instances store operation sequence in its own *oplog* , if a slave falls too far behind the state of the master, it cannot "catchup" and must re-sync from scratch.

Slave may become out of sync with a master if:

- The slave falls far behind the data updates available from that master.

- The slave stops for some reason and restarts later after the master has overwritten the relevant operations from the master.

Once master comes back up we will need to resync the oplog of slave with master. To do a resync execute *replSetSyncFrom* command

```
> { replSetSyncFrom: "ip-172-31-63-100:27017" }

ip-172-31-63-100:27017

> rs.printSlaveReplicationInfo()

source: ip-172-31-63-100:27017

     syncedTo: Thu Jun 18 2015 11:20:31 GMT+0000 (UTC)

secs (0 hrs) behind the freshest member
```

Alternate way to do a resync of slave is to stop and restart the slave with - -*autoresync* option.

Please use *resync* frugally and only when absolutely needed. *resync* is a costly operation, the cost will be determined by how far behind the slave has fallen from master.

"Out of sync" conditions are distressing for replication and when slaves become out of sync replication stops. If this occurs, manual intervention from Administrators may be needed. To mitigate these issues, larger oplog should be specified during start of master instance.

To start master with the desired *oplogsize* , start with setting --- *oplogSize*

```
> Mongod --master --oplogSize  <size>
```

Master slave replication is a good solution but it does not provide redundancy and failover, replica set is a better solution (next chapter talks about replica sets) that provides everything master slave replication provides and then some.

Templated Deployment

What we did in the previous sections was to set up the EC2 resource manually by choosing all the steps using the wizard. For high availability and durability of applications, these resources need to be deployed in multiple regions. if we have to replicate this multiple times , more time is spent in managing these deployments and admin tasks, rather than doing the actual development.

AWS cloud formation is a service that helps manage AWS resources by leveraging reusable templates. Templated approach is repeatable and consistent way of managing your deployment on AWS.

The building blocks of cloud formation are templates and stacks (*figure 3.1*).

Templates are blueprints of your resource properties and stack is the actual implementation of your template wherein the resources described are actually provisioned.

Template is a file with format compatible with JSON standards. To launch the resources described in template we package our template in logical unit called stack.

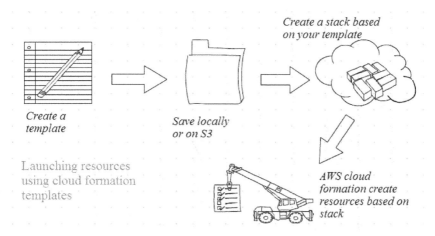

Figure 3.1

Templates can be overwhelming initially, to get yourself started please refer *aws.amazon.com* for sample templates.

http://docs.aws.amazon.com/AWSCloudFormation/latest/UserGuide/cf n-sample-templates.html

For this deployment we will use a preconfigured cloud template to launch a Development *MongoDB* instance with replica set containing a single member.

It also has options for creating replica sets and shards (we will look at these concepts in subsequent chapters).

MongoDB on AWS

Go to *"AWS console home → cloud formation"*

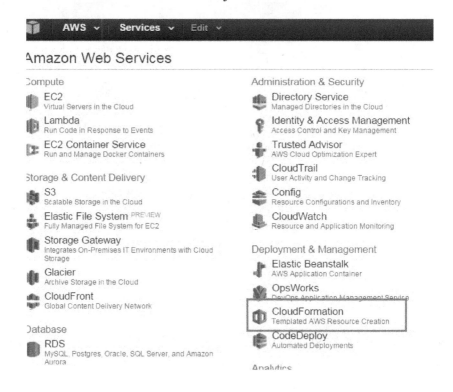

1. Click on Create stack on the next page
2. Provide any name (we used *AWSMongoDB*) of the stack and in the specify an amazon S3 template URL provide the following *https://s3.amazonaws.com/quickstart-reference/mongodb/latest/templates/MongoDB-VPC.template*

MongoDB on AWS

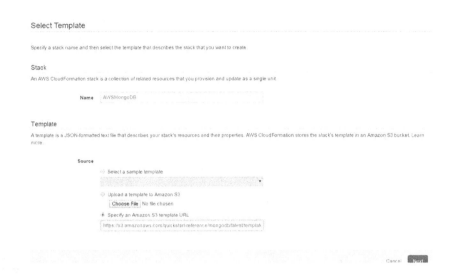

Click on next

3. In the next screen , keep the replica set count to 1 , since we are launching a dev instance. Also keep the shards to 0 for the time being

MongoDB on AWS

4. You will also need to choose the key name , choose the existing key

5. On the next screen click on create , this will create the template
6. You should see a plethora of activity going on in *Events* tab .

Give it few minutes to complete.

7. Create complete screen confirms , stack creation is complete

Navigate to EC2 console home , you should see two instances running with only one instance displaying the IP address . The instance that shows Public DNS is the EC2 instance with Network Address Translation (NAT) , we discuss what exactly is this NAT in the section that follows.[3]

---

[3] To feed the George inside you refer this interesting article on how NAT actually works http://computer.howstuffworks.com/nat.htm

8. Using putty connect to your MongoDB linux instance via NAT. Default user id for amazon linux instance is ec2-user

Connecting to Instance inside private subnet

This deployment is an example of a private subnet cluster topology. This topology uses a NAT instance with an associated Elastic IP Address (EIP) and a security group that allows SSH traffic to the NAT instance.

Amazon EC2 instances that serve as *MongoDB* node is created inside the private subnet. This topology does not allow the Amazon EC2 instances within the *MongoDB* cluster direct access to the Internet or to other AWS services. Instead, their access is routed through the NAT instance that resides in the public subnet.

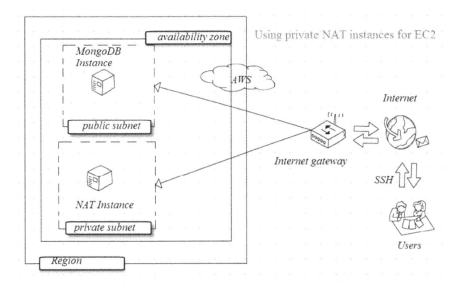

1. Go to AWS console home, right click on the instance you need to connect to , and click on connect.

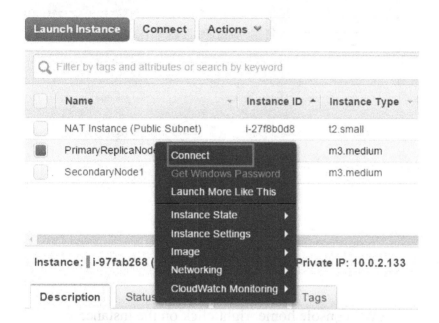

2. The pop will show the private IP of your instance and example SSH command , copy the example displayed

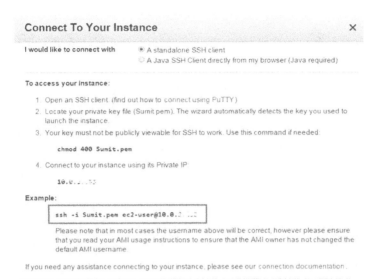

3. Launch your NAT instance and log into root user , try to execute the ssh command

   Ex : *ssh –i <your private key> ec2-user@ip-address*

   Place your .pem file at /home/ec2-user , If you don't have the file available , you might encounter the following errors

Warning: Identity file <your key name> not accessible: No such file or directory

Or

Permission denied (publickey).

Make sure the key is having read only permissions , else ssh will fail with below error

```
@@@@@@@@@@@@@@@@@@@@@@@@@@@@@@@@@@@@@@@
@@@@@@@@@@@@@@@@@@@@@@@@@@@@

@        WARNING: UNPROTECTED PRIVATE KEY FILE!

@@@@@@@@@@@@@@@@@@@@@@@@@@@@@@@@@@@@@@@
@@@@@@@@@@@@@@@@@@@@@@@@@@@@

Permissions 0644 for 'Sumit.pem' are too open.

It is required that your private key files are NOT accessible by others.

This private key will be ignored.

bad permissions: ignore key: Sumit.pem

Permission denied (publickey).
```

Starting Mongod

1. Start the Mongod process

```
sudo service mongod start
```

2. Check the contents of log file
   at */var/log/mongodb/mongod.log*

3. Check the status of MongoDB services by executing the
   following command
   ps -edaf | grep mongo

```
[root@ip-10-0-1-49 bin]# ps -edaf | grep mongo
mongod     2138      1  0 12:03 ?       00:00:02 /usr/bin/mongod -f /etc/mongod.conf
root       2353   2275  0 12:17 pts/0   00:00:00 grep mongo
[root@ip-10-0-1-49 bin]#
```

4. All your data is going to /var/lib/mongo in the current install

Data directory-*Under the hood*

If you look at data directory you would notice plethora of files, a directory named journal and *mogod.lock* file. let's try to understand significance of some of the important ones, and what these files and directories are doing here.

Name space file- In the data directory you will find **.ns** file for each database. A namespace corresponds to metadata of a collection. Each database is organized into namespace. The document for each collection is grouped into their own namespace files. Look at **.ns** file as big hash table where entries about a collection or index are created. Collection namespace contains metadata concerning Name of the collection, count of collection, index details et al.

Journal – we will talk about journals in detail when we discuss storage considerations (***Chapter 6***). For now think of Journaling as *MongoDB's* way of logging the writes that can be replayed in case server crashes in between the writes. Think of it as *MongoDB's* attempt to make write operations more durable from abnormal system shutdowns.

This directory will be empty right now since we didn't enable journaling in the current run.

Mongod.lock – This file will be present when you run mongod without journaling, as is the case in our current *MongoDB* instance.

After a graceful *MongoDB* shutdown this file will be automatically deleted, this is a flag for mongod at startup that the last shutdown was clean.

If we find this file when restarting mongod, we will need to repair our data before mongod starts again.

If we had an abnormal shutdown during the last run , we can repair *MongoDB* instance either via *mongodump*.

```
[ec2-user ~]$ mongodump --repair
```

Or ,via mongod's inherent repair option, start mongod with *--repair* option

```
[ec2-user ~]$ mongod --dbpath /data --repair
```

***Configuration file* :**When we start our DB instance it triggers */etc/init.d/mongod* or */etc/rc.d/mongod* that makes use of a configuration file located at */etc/mongod.conf.d* to start the mongod with the appropriate configuration parameters.

Some of the common configuration parameters are explained below

MongoDB on AWS

Fork : if set to true enables a daemon mode for mongod, which forks the MongoDB from the current session and runs the database as a conventional server.

Port : Set to 27017 by default. This is the listener port MongoDB uses for database instances. MongoDB can bind to any port. For running more than one mongod process give separate port numbers.

dbPath: set to */var/lib/data*, which specifies where MongoDB will store its data files. The user account for mongod will need read and write access to this directory.

systemLog.path : set to */var/log/mongodb/mongod.log*. This is where mongod will write its output. If not set, mongod writes all output to standard output (e.g. stdout.)

storage.journal.enabled: If set to true, allows journaling. Journaling ensures single instance write-durability. This setting is no redundant as 64-bit builds of mongod enable journaling by default.

replSet: If defined allows the mongod instance to run as a replication set member

We launched an EC2 instance using manual and templated deployment, we left the discussion on EC2 instance family , and which instance family will be fit our needs of running a *MongoDB* database. let's look at some of the selection criteria for suitable EC2 instance.

RAM considerations

From cost perspective RAM would probably be the costliest hardware procured during instance provisioning. What determines how much RAM we need for *MongoDB*? *MongoDB* stores a subset of the most frequently used data in RAM , this is done to minimize time spent on disk seek operations and allows mongoDB to service client applications faster. If the information client application is seeking is not in memory *MongoDB* will start paging to disk to make room for data that was requested and was not found in the disk ("page faults").

We can imagine what will happen if the RAM capacity is not big enough and *MongoDB* constantly spends time on "page faults", it will be spending more time in page faults than servicing the clients (*figure 3.2*).

MongoDB uses Least recently used algorithm for page faults, the data that was not recently used is bumped off by server to make space for something that was recently requested from the disk.

When we use on premise servers we need to estimate the optimal RAM size that we will need in foreseeable future. getting it just right needs some skill and experience , we can always get more than necessary with the risk of overspending on something we will never use.

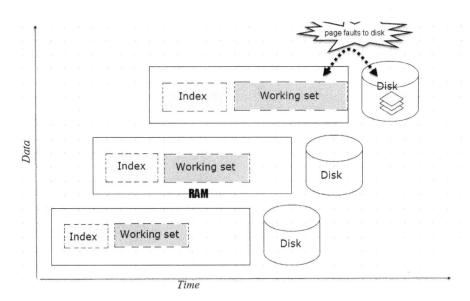

Figure 3.2

This risk of overspending is mitigated when we launch resources on cloud. The resources we provision are "on-demand", we can always downgrade or upgrade our RAM by going for a bigger instance in the same family. Once your *MongoDB* cluster is up and running we can look at some key statistics to gauge if the RAM we have is able to scale up to operational demands.

We can use the the workingset command to get details on RAM usage

```
db.runCommand({ serverStatus: 1, workingSet: 1}). workingSet
```

Below are some statistics *workingset* command will throw at us, we can get a pulse check on how our instances are doing with the current workload.

pagesInMemory: The value in this field give the number of pages Mongo loaded in the memory. Each page is roughly 4KB in size,to come to a space estimate multiply this number with 4KB and you get the size of pages residing in memory. Initially pagesInMemory*4 is your total database size . it increases overtime and when it reaches the threshold limit for RAM memory remains static.

computationTimeMicros: The value in this field gives how much time in microseconds server spent to give the working set statistics on console. Working set command should be used with caution it takes some server resources to get the stats back.

overSeconds : Time difference in seconds between the oldest page and the newest page loaded by Mongo in the memory. A large value for this entry indicates the pages are remaining longer in the RAM , a shorter value indicates more page faults. If you find a decrease in this value means mongo is getting constant request for the data not residing in memory .When the server is started, this value will obviously be less but eventually, with more data being accessed with time, more pages will be loaded by Mongo in the memory.

AWS instance selection

MongoDB systems are memory and I/O bound and rarely need high CPU machines. AWS provides

Here are some EC2 family and instance types that can be used for mongoDB instances. Please note these are just general guidelines please refer AWS catalogue for what family and instance will best fit your needs.

> ***General-Purpose (M3 instance types)*** - This family provides a balance of CPU, memory, and network resources making them a good choice for mongoDB replica sets. This resource family is an ideal choice for running small and mid-size MongoDB deployments that require scalable memory and CPU hungry applications .M3 Instances provide the option of a larger number of virtual CPUs for higher performance.

> ***Micro Instances***. Micro, or T1, instances provide very small CPU resources at very low price. They are well suited for use as arbiter members in replica set. Arbiter does not need to store data from primary. Arbiter only becomes "active" during primary elections.

> ***Compute-Optimized***. This family includes the C1 and CC2 instance types, and is geared towards applications that benefit from high CPU power. These instances have a higher ratio of

vCPUs to memory .when it comes to CPU cost these have the lowest cost per vCPU among all the Amazon EC2 instance types generally speaking MongoDB rarely require high CPU bandwidth. Most mongoDB operations requirements center on high memory and I/Unless the working set rarely changes you should always go for higher memory.

Memory-Optimized. Instance types of his family are designed for memory-intensive client applications. They have the lowest cost of RAM among all EC2 instance types. They are well suited for high performance distributed databases (specially *MongoDB*).if you have a busy cluster high memory will server you best , server can get the results from working set in RAM if you have higher memory capacity.

*Storage Optimized (I2).*This family provides very high I/O performance by making use of SSD backed instance storage. The only downside is for performance you are relying on ephemeral storage, so backup strategy needs to complement the volatile storage. They are a nice fit for transactional operations that may require scaling the I/O and high network packet rate per second.

You don't need to be right the first time

Cloud platforms like AWS provides freedom to resize our hardware infrastructure if your need changes. If we find that *m3.Large* best fits our needs,instead of *m3.medium* as originally selected, we can upgrade. The only limitation when resizing is whether your root volume is ephemeral or EBS backed. If the root volume is EBS backed you can easily resize the instance by changing the instance type. With root volume in ephemeral store you will have to do an explicit migration to the new instance. It's recommended (if your wallet allows), to use EBS volumes for root volumes.

Another limitation when resizing your instances is virtualization compatibility .AWS uses two kinds of virtualization paravirtual (PV) and hardware virtual machine (HVM).these two virtualizations are mutually exclusive, we cannot change the virtualization type of the instance and cannot resize to an instance with a different virtualization type.

MongoDB operations Log (opLog)

Before we deep dive into replication in the forthcoming chapter, lets learn a bit more about opLog. MongoDB needs to keep track of what operations are being performed on primary , this information is important from replication set perspective as it tells the secondary members reading from primary the chronological order of events on primary. To accomplish the goal of keeping this metadata MongoDB uses a capped collection known as oplog (operations log) that keeps a rolling record of all operations that modify the data stored in your databases. A capped collection means any new operations arriving at the collection will automatically move the old collection thus keeping the size of the collection manageable.

MongoDB records all operations it performs on the primary on the primary's oplog. The secondary members then infuse and apply these operations in an asynchronous process, and store them in thelocal.oplog.rs collection. Primary member is not the only source for Oplog sync activity, all replica set members send heartbeats (pings) to all other members. Any member can import oplog entries from any other member (regardless of its status of Primary or Secondary member).

Every operation in the oplog is idempotent, what does that means , it's a mathematical term roughly translated to "whenever it is applied twice to any value, it gives the same result as if it were applied once". Another important property of oplog is it does not store any operations that do not change the data, for example queries or DML statements won't be stored in oplog.

Oplog Sizing

MongoDB creates an oplog of a default size during initialization; the default size will vary depending on your operating system. By default for 64 Bit Linux lower of 5% of the available free space or 1 GB will be used.

i.e. if 5% of your free space is more than 1 GB that will be used else 1 GB will be used as default opLog size.prior to mongod creates an oplog, its size can be specified using the *oplogSizeMB* option. By default, the size of the oplog is as follows:

> For 64-bit Linux, Solaris, FreeBSD, and Windows systems, MongoDB allocates 5% of the available free disk space, but will always allocate at least 1 gigabyte and never more than 50 gigabytes.

Oplog sizing imperatives.

OpLog size is directly proportional to number of writes application performs, if your applications are write heavy you might need a larger opLog .similarly a read heavy application with minimal writes may require smaller opLog.

Below are few workloads that might warrant a larger oplog.

- o Updates to Multiple Documents at Once- multi-updates may need to be translated into individual operations in order to maintain idempotency. This requires larger oplog size
- o Significant Number of In-Place Updates-for obvious reasons If a significant portion of the workload is updates it may require larger oplog to record large number of database operations (but does not change the quantity of data on disk)

o Equal Deletes and Inserts-If you delete roughly the same amount of data as you insert, the size of the operation log can be quite large.

In a standalone *MongoDB* deployment that we just saw there is no redundancy of data. It's good for POC or non-prod environments. To provide a highly available system data and systems should have redundancy and high distribution. To achieve that *MongoDB* provides two functionalities replication and sharding. Let's discuss replication first and we will move from a bare bones replication known as master slave replication to a better solution known as replica set.

Chapter 4

MongoDB Cluster-Replica set

Chapter Objectives

➤ *MongoDB replica-set and why they are needed*

➤ *Deploying three member replica set using cloud formation template*

➤ *Use case for different Replica set members*

➤ *Replication under the hood , replication lag and write concerns*

➤ *Replica set members across AWS availability zones and regions*

....

C lustering in layman's term is confederation of servers to make them appear as a single server to client applications. Clustered configuration for databases provides applications with continuity (High availability and fault tolerance), scalability, and performance.

A database cluster should have the following fundamental properties.

- *Client applications should not feel any difference while interacting with the cluster, cluster look and feel should feel exactly like networking with a single server.*
- *Applications running inside the cluster should not need any modifications to make them run inside the cluster.*
- *Contributing Nodes inside the cluster should not be aware they are part of a cluster. Failure of one node should have no adverse effect on the other peers inside the cluster.*
- *There should be no need to modify the server OS to make it work with other nodes inside a cluster.*

In *MongoDB* clustering is achieved through replica set, a replica set satisfies all the aforementioned requirements of a database cluster. Replica sets in cluster are modeled on shared nothing configuration, thus each node acts independently from other with separate storage for each member of the replica set. Data redundancy is established to facilitate automatic recovery and continuity in case any member goes down inside the replica set.

MongoDB Replica Set

Replica sets provide the data redundancy and failover mechanism for *MongoDB* clusters. Replication provides an effective mechanism in case the host server is unresponsive due to network partition or any other hardware failure. Replication can also provide better data locality

MongoDB Cluster-Replica set

by maintaining data in different availability zones or regions, nearest to client applications.

MongoDB allows routing of read/write operations to be sent to different servers, thus allowing data locality by allowing clients to send requests to the region nearest to them.

A replica set in MongoDB is a group of mongod processes that provide redundancy and high availability. A replica set consists of at least a Primary and secondary member(s).

Primary Member- The primary receives all write operations.

Secondary Member -replicate operations from the primary to maintain an identical data set.

To put it in simple terms replication can be viewed as a two-step process.

Step 1: Master (Primary) mongod goes down, secondary server takes up as primary and becomes the new Primary

Step 2: When old Primary Mongod is back online it becomes the new Secondary.

For practical reasons there cannot be just one primary and one secondary member in replication set, we will look that why it doesn't make sense. At a minimum MongoDB replication set requires 3 members, one primary and two secondary members (*figure 4.1*) .

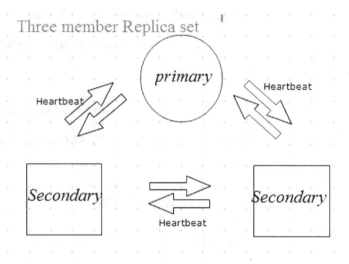

Figure 4.1

Three member replica sets provide enough redundancy to survive most network partitions and other system failures. There is an upper limit on maximum members allowed as well, replication set cannot have more than 12 members.

Let's look at members of replica set in detail before we create one.

Primary : This is where all write operation for replica set go, there can be only one Primary in a replica set. Writes going to primary member are cascaded down to secondary members later.

MongoDB Cluster-Replica set

Secondary :Secondary member maintains an identical data set as primary by replicating data. Secondary members based on their priority and election by their peers can also become primary members (*figure 4.2*) , if circumstances arise due to failure of original Primary. There can be (and should be for reasons for redundancy) more than one secondary member in replica set.

Secondary members can be configured in multiple ways based on usage criteria and application needs.

Ex : If the objective is to create a secondary member that will serve as cold standby in a data center we can classify a secondary member as hidden members (more on this , in sections that follow)

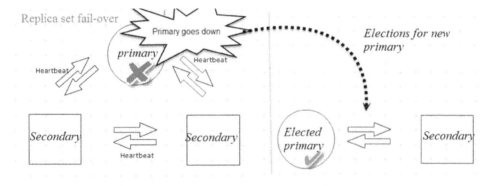

Figure 4.2

Deployment Scenarios

Three Member Replica set

MongoDB Cluster-Replica set

MongoDB on AWS

In the last chapter we launched a standalone MongoDB EC2 instance along with a NAT instance , we will launch a three member replica set using the same template.

The template can be found on S3

https://s3.amazonaws.com/quickstart-reference/mongodb/latest/templates/MongoDB-VPC.template

When using the template create the stack ,keep the *ClusterReplicaSetCount* parameter to 3 and *ClusterShardCount* to 0.

Parameters

BuildBucket	quickstart-reference/mongodb/latest	Main Bucket where 1
ClusterReplicaSetCount	1	Number of Replica S
ClusterShardCount	0	Number of Shards [C

MongoDB Cluster-Replica set

MongoDB on AWS

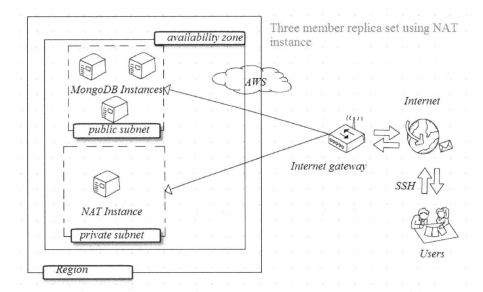

Figure 4.3

Once you launch create the stack, three linux instances will be launched with *MongoDB* installed (*figure 4.3*).

Let's look at detailed steps to get our replica set up and running

1. Create new directory */data/db* on each linux instance , the directory will be our data store
2. We will be creating a new replica set and name it rs3
3. Stop any mongod daemons if still running on all three instances

```
$ sudo service mongod stop
```

4. If you haven't already noticed when you start your instance the mongod deamon starts with a config file.

```
[ec2-user@n1.mongo.com ~]$ ps -ef | grep mongo

mongod   2224   1 0 12:54 ?      00:00:02 /usr/bin/mongod -f
/etc/mongod.conf

ec2-user 2704 2572 0 13:03 pts/0   00:00:00 grep mongo
```

To invoke mongod with the new replica set every time the server restarts,we will modify the config file with the replica set details

5. Sudo as root and open the file */etc/mongod.conf* , if you are using the sample cloud formation template the instances arrive with all the necessary entries to start replica set .

Since we modified the data path and replica set name we would need to refer the new path in the configuration file.

There are two entries we need to modify

a. *db path* : if set to dbpath=/var/lib/mongo , comment it and add another entry dbpath=/data/db

b. *replSet*: If you want to rename your replica set comment the entry and add another entry replSet=<Your replica set name>

MongoDB on AWS

Note : To use the existing entries defined in the config file , make sure you repeat the steps of replica set initialization and adding the nodes to it with the correct replica set.

6. Start the mongod with replication set option, give the same name as defined in the *replSet* entry

```
$ mongod --replSet "rs3"
```

Note: Use the same name as defined in file /etc/mongod.conf

7. We should see the following message , indicating mongod stated successfully

```
2015-06-10T10:51:25.528+0000 I NETWORK  [initandlisten] waiting for
connections on port 27017
```

8. Login to any member and start mongo shell and initiate replication

```
> rs.initiatc()
{
```

```
        "info2" : "no configuration explicitly specified -- making one",

        "me" : "ip-10-0-4-121:27017",

        "ok" : 1

    }
```

9. Add the other two members of the replica set

```
rs3:PRIMARY> rs.add("10.0.3.xxx")

{ "ok" : 1 }

rs3:PRIMARY> rs.add("10.x.2.xx")

{ "ok" : 1 }
```

10. Check the replica set configuration using rs.conf(), we should see three instances .

```
rs3:PRIMARY> rs.conf()

{

    "_id" : "rs3",

    "version" : 3,

    "members" : [
```

MongoDB on AWS

```
{
        "_id" : 0,
        "host" : "ip-xx-x-x-xxx:27017",
        "arbiterOnly" : false,
        "buildIndexes" : true,
        "hidden" : false,
        "priority" : 1,
        "tags" : {

        },
        "slaveDelay" : 0,
        "votes" : 1
},
{
        "_id" : 1,
        "host" : "1x.0.3.xxx:27017",
        "arbiterOnly" : false,
        "buildIndexes" : true,
        "hidden" : false,
        "priority" : 1,
        "tags" : {
```

MongoDB Cluster-Replica set

```
            },
            "slaveDelay" : 0,
            "votes" : 1
        },
        {

            "_id" : 2,
            "host" : "1x.0.x.xx:27017",
            "arbiterOnly" : false,
            "buildIndexes" : true,
            "hidden" : false,
            "priority" : 1,
            "tags" : {

            },
            "slaveDelay" : 0,
            "votes" : 1
        }
    ],
    "settings" : {
        "chainingAllowed" : true,
```

MongoDB Cluster-Replica set

```
            "heartbeatTimeoutSecs" : 10,

            "getLastErrorModes" : {



            },

            "getLastErrorDefaults" : {

                "w" : 1,

                "wtimeout" : 0

            }

        }

    }

    rs3:PRIMARY>
```

11. Using *rs.status()* method we can validate which node is the primary member and which one is the secondary , This method is also a quick way to check the replication status.

```
rs3:PRIMARY> rs.status()

{

    "set" : "rs3",

    "date" : ISODate("2015-06-10T10:57:56.701Z"),

    "myState" : 1,
```

```
"members" : [
        {
                "_id" : 0,
                "name" : "ip-10-0-4-xxx:27017",
                "health" : 1,
                "state" : 1,
                "stateStr" : "PRIMARY",
                "uptime" : 408,
                "optime" : Timestamp(1433933821, 1),
                "optimeDate" : ISODate("2015-06-10T10:57:01Z"),
                "electionTime" : Timestamp(1433933704, 2),
                "electionDate" : ISODate("2015-06-10T10:55:04Z"),
                "configVersion" : 3,
                "self" : true
        },
        {
                "_id" : 1,
                "name" : "10.0.3.xxx:27017",
                "health" : 1,
                "state" : 2,
                "stateStr" : "SECONDARY",
```

MongoDB Cluster-Replica set

"uptime" : 77,

"optime" : Timestamp(1433933821, 1),

"optimeDate" : ISODate("2015-06-10T10:57:01Z"),

"lastHeartbeat" : ISODate("2015-06-10T10:57:55.916Z"),

"lastHeartbeatRecv" : ISODate("2015-06-10T10:57:55.211Z"),

"pingMs" : 1,

"syncingTo" : "ip-10-0-4-xxx:27017",

"configVersion" : 3
},
{

"_id" : 2,

"name" : "10.0.2.xx:27017",

"health" : 1,

"state" : 2,

"stateStr" : "SECONDARY",

"uptime" : 54,

"optime" : Timestamp(1433933821, 1),

"optimeDate" : ISODate("2015-06-10T10:57:01Z"),

"lastHeartbeat" : ISODate("2015-06-10T10:57:55.933Z"),

"lastHeartbeatRecv" : ISODate("2015-06-10T10:57:55.951Z"),

MongoDB Cluster-Replica set

```
                "pingMs" : 1,

                "syncingTo" : "ip-10-0-4-xxx:27017",

                "configVersion" : 3

            }

        ],

        "ok" : 1

    }
```

HA in action

Before we wander deep into replica set , let's look at how *MongoDB* replication configured on AWS is able to gracefully make a switch to an available secondary instance .

To recap what we have accomplished so far, we have a three member replica set with each member in a separate AWS availability zone.

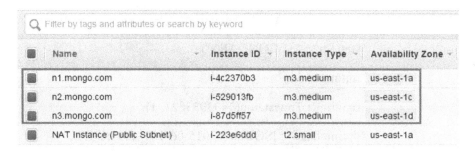

All three instances are launched in US East region on Zones 1a, 1c and 1d respectively.

MongoDB Cluster-Replica set

MongoDB on AWS

1. Log into mongo shell and look at the replica set status once
   again, for ease of identification I have replaced the names in the
   below snapshots to resemble the tags in AWS console.
   Node *n1.mongo.com* is primary whereas *n2.mongo.com* and
   n3.mongo.com are secondary members of our replica set.

```
s-1-rs:SECONDARY> rs.status()
{
     "set" : "s-1-rs",
     "date" : ISODate("2015-06-11T12:47:55.899Z"),
     "myState" : 2,
     "members" : [
          {
               "_id" : 0,
               "name" : "n1.mongo.com:27017",
               "health" : 1,
               "state" : 1,
               "stateStr" : "PRIMARY",
               "uptime" : 643,
               "optime" : Timestamp(1433973956, 1),
               "optimeDate" : ISODate("2015-06-10T22:05:56Z"),
               "lastHeartbeat" : ISODate("2015-06-11T12:47:55.238Z"),
```

MongoDB Cluster-Replica set

```
                    "lastHeartbeatRecv" : ISODate("2015-06-
11T12:47:54.830Z"),

                    "pingMs" : 1,

                    "electionTime" : Timestamp(1434026149, 1),

                    "electionDate" : ISODate("2015-06-11T12:35:49Z"),

                    "configVersion" : 15

            },

            {

                "_id" : 1,

                "name" : "n3.mongo.com:27017",

                "health" : 1,

                "state" : 2,

                "stateStr" : "SECONDARY",

                "uptime" : 729,

                "optime" : Timestamp(1433973956, 1),

                "optimeDate" : ISODate("2015-06-10T22:05:56Z"),

                "configVersion" : 15,

                "self" : true

            },

            {

                "_id" : 2,
```

MongoDB Cluster-Replica set

```
              "name" : "n2.mongo.com:27017",

              "health" : 1,

              "state" : 2,

              "stateStr" : "SECONDARY",

              "uptime" : 643,

              "optime" : Timestamp(1433973956, 1),

              "optimeDate" : ISODate("2015-06-10T22:05:56Z"),

              "lastHeartbeat" : ISODate("2015-06-11T12:47:54.881Z"),

              "lastHeartbeatRecv" : ISODate("2015-06-
11T12:47:54.419Z"),

              "pingMs" : 0,

              "configVersion" : 15

          }

      ],

      "ok" : 1

}
```

2. Due to network outage in zone us-east-1a , our primary member is unavailable , let's stop the instance *n1.mongo.com* from AWS console for a moment

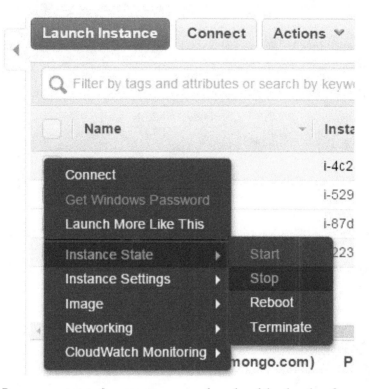

3. Issue *rs.status()* once more to do a health check of our replica set, you would notice *n1.mongo.com* is "not reachable" and members have elected *n3.mongo.com* as the new primary.

```
rs.status()
{
    "set" : "s-1-rs",
    "date" : ISODate("2015-06-11T13:01:34.395Z"),
    "myState" : 1,
```

MongoDB Cluster-Replica set

```
    "members" : [
        {
            "_id" : 0,
            "name" : "n1.mongo.com:27017",
            "health" : 0,
            "state" : 8,
            "stateStr" : "(not reachable/healthy)",
            "uptime" : 0,
            "optime" : Timestamp(0, 0),
            "optimeDate" : ISODate("1970-01-01T00:00:00Z"),
            "lastHeartbeat" : ISODate("2015-06-11T13:01:34.354Z"),
            "lastHeartbeatRecv" : ISODate("2015-06-
11T13:01:11.789Z"),
            "pingMs" : 2,
            "lastHeartbeatMessage" : "Failed attempt to connect to
n1.mongo.com:27017; couldn't connect to server n1.mongo.com:27017
(10.0.2.29), connection attempt failed",
            "configVersion" : -1
        },
        {
            "_id" : 1,
            "name" : "n3.mongo.com:27017",
```

MongoDB Cluster-Replica set

```
            "health" : 1,

            "state" : 1,

            "stateStr" : "PRIMARY",

            "uptime" : 1548,

            "optime" : Timestamp(1433973956, 1),

            "optimeDate" : ISODate("2015-06-10T22:05:56Z"),

            "electionTime" : Timestamp(1434027675, 1),

            "electionDate" : ISODate("2015-06-11T13:01:15Z"),

            "configVersion" : 15,

            "self" : true

    },
    {

        "_id" : 2,

        "name" : "n2.mongo.com:27017",

        "health" : 1,

        "state" : 2,

        "stateStr" : "SECONDARY",

        "uptime" : 1461,

        "optime" : Timestamp(1433973956, 1),

        "optimeDate" : ISODate("2015-06-10T22:05:56Z"),

        "lastHeartbeat" : ISODate("2015-06-11T13:01:33.470Z"),
```

MongoDB Cluster-Replica set

```
                    "lastHeartbeatRecv" : ISODate("2015-06-
11T13:01:32.967Z"),

                    "pingMs" : 0,

                    "configVersion" : 15

            }

        ],

        "ok" : 1

}
```

why n3.mongo.com was chosen as the new primary and not n2.mongo.com. It's a valid question , there is a lot that goes into electing a new primary. Let park this question for few pages, we will discuss elections later in the chapter.

4. Go back to AWS EC2 home and restart *n1.mongo.com*, you would notice it joins the replica set as a secondary member.

```
s-1-rs:PRIMARY> rs.status()
{
    "set" : "s-1-rs",

    "date" : ISODate("2015-06-11T13:07:16.968Z"),

    "myState" : 1,

    "members" : [
```

```
{
        "_id" : 0,
        "name" : "n1.mongo.com:27017",
        "health" : 1,
        "state" : 2,
        "stateStr" : "SECONDARY",
        "uptime" : 88,
        "optime" : Timestamp(1433973956, 1),
        "optimeDate" : ISODate("2015-06-10T22:05:56Z"),
        "lastHeartbeat" : ISODate("2015-06-11T13:07:16.756Z"),
        "lastHeartbeatRecv" : ISODate("2015-06-
11T13:07:15.666Z"),
        "pingMs" : 1,
        "configVersion" : 15
    },
    {
        "_id" : 1,
        "name" : "n3.mongo.com:27017",
        "health" : 1,
        "state" : 1,
        "stateStr" : "PRIMARY",
```

MongoDB Cluster-Replica set

```
                "uptime" : 1890,

                "optime" : Timestamp(1433973956, 1),

                "optimeDate" : ISODate("2015-06-10T22:05:56Z"),

                "electionTime" : Timestamp(1434027675, 1),

                "electionDate" : ISODate("2015-06-11T13:01:15Z"),

                "configVersion" : 15,

                "self" : true

        },

        {

                "_id" : 2,

                "name" : "n2.mongo.com:27017",

                "health" : 1,

                "state" : 2,

                "stateStr" : "SECONDARY",

                "uptime" : 1804,

                "optime" : Timestamp(1433973956, 1),

                "optimeDate" : ISODate("2015-06-10T22:05:56Z"),

                "lastHeartbeat" : ISODate("2015-06-11T13:07:16.376Z"),

                "lastHeartbeatRecv" : ISODate("2015-06-
11T13:07:15.192Z"),

                "pingMs" : 1,
```

```
                    "configVersion" : 15

              }

        ],

        "ok" : 1

    }
```

What we just demonstrated and tested was the automatic failover mechanism of replica set and how MongoDB was functional even with a replica set member unavailable.

Priority 0 Replica Set Members

Priority 0 replica set members can participate in the election process (*figure 4.4*), can accept read requests from client applications but can never become primary themselves in case of primary going down.

- o One of the objectives of having these members is to serve as cold standbys.
- o They also serve in filling the voting quorum in case of election process, to choose the primary for quick failover.
- o Priority 0 members cannot trigger election but play an important role in setups involving nodes of varying hardware capabilities and geographic spreads. These

members assist in making sure that that only competent secondary member becomes a primary.

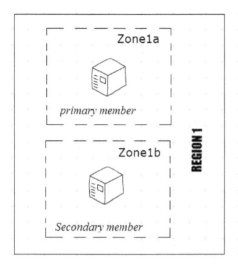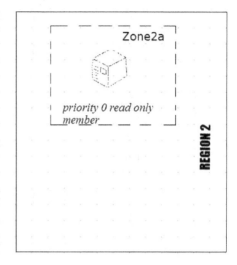

Priority 0 replica set member

Figure 4.4

If objective is to prevent applications from reading from a secondary member, to allow them to serve "dirty reads" for reporting systems, classify the member as Hidden member instead.

Setting priority of a replica set member

1. Connect to primary using mongo shell and execute *rs.conf()* command. The *rs.conf()* method returns a replica set configuration document that contains the current configuration for a replica set. Document returned by this method contains

a member's field which contains an array of member configuration documents, each document correspond to single member of the replica set.

```
s-1-rs:PRIMARY> cfg = rs.conf()
{
    "_id" : "s-1-rs",
    "version" : 9,
    "members" : [
        {
            "_id" : 0,
            "host" : "n1.mongo.com:27017",
            "arbiterOnly" : false,
            "buildIndexes" : true,
            "hidden" : false,
            "priority" : 1,
            "tags" : {
            },
            "slaveDelay" : 0,
            "votes" : 1
        },
        {
```

MongoDB on AWS

```
            "_id" : 1,

            "host" : "n3.mongo.com:27017",

            "arbiterOnly" : false,

            "buildIndexes" : true,

            "hidden" : false,

            "priority" : 1,

            "tags" : {

            },

            "slaveDelay" : 0,

            "votes" : 1

        },

        {

            "_id" : 2,

            "host" : "n2.mongo.com:27017",

            "arbiterOnly" : false,

            "buildIndexes" : true,

            "hidden" : false,

            "priority" : 1,

            "tags" : {


            },
```

```
                "slaveDelay" : 0,

                "votes" : 1

            }

    ],

    "settings" : {

        "chainingAllowed" : true,

        "heartbeatTimeoutSecs" : 10,

        "getLastErrorModes" : {


        },

        "getLastErrorDefaults" : {

            "w" : 1,

            "wtimeout" : 0

        }

    }

}
```

2. Using the array result from *rs.conf()* invocation , downgrade the priority of any member using their position in array.

```
s-1-rs:PRIMARY> cfg.members[2].priority = 0
```

3. The configuration change does trigger a change till we reconfigure the replica set. *rs.reconfig()* method is used to reconfigure the replica set with the updated replica set configuration document.

```
s-1-rs:PRIMARY> rs.reconfig(cfg)

{ "ok" : 1 }
```

4. Check the priority of host with id=2 , it's now a read only member of replica set.

```
s-1-rs:PRIMARY> rs.conf()
{
        "_id" : "s-1-rs",
        "version" : 10,
        "members" : [
                {
                        "_id" : 0,
                        "host" : "n1.mongo.com:27017",
                        "arbiterOnly" : false,
                        "buildIndexes" : true,
```

```json
        "hidden" : false,
        "priority" : 1,
        "tags" : {

        },
        "slaveDelay" : 0,
        "votes" : 1
    },
    {

        "_id" : 1,
        "host" : "n3.mongo.com:27017",
        "arbiterOnly" : false,
        "buildIndexes" : true,
        "hidden" : false,
        "priority" : 1,
        "tags" : {

        },
        "slaveDelay" : 0,
        "votes" : 1
    },
```

```
        {
            "_id" : 2,
            "host" : "n2.mongo.com:27017",
            "arbiterOnly" : false,
            "buildIndexes" : true,
            "hidden" : false,
            "priority" : 0,
            "tags" : {

            },
            "slaveDelay" : 0,
            "votes" : 1
        }
    ],
    "settings" : {
        "chainingAllowed" : true,
        "heartbeatTimeoutSecs" : 10,
        "getLastErrorModes" : {

        },
        "getLastErrorDefaults" : {
```

MongoDB Cluster-Replica set

```
            "w" : 1,

            "wtimeout" : 0

        }

    }

}
```

Hidden Replica Set Members.

A hidden member is a priority 0 member again, these members maintain a copy of the primary's data set but is also invisible to client applications.

What's the use of having a hidden member? They are good candidates for workloads that differ from other members of replica set.

These members can be useful for exclusively dedicating them for reporting needs , thereby restricting any unnecessary reads on the system other than

Configuring a hidden member of replica set

The steps to make a member hidden are almost similar as priority 0 members

1. Assign the priority to 0 for the desired member, followed by setting the hidden setting to true

```
s-1-rs:PRIMARY> cfg.members[2].priority = 0

0

s-1-rs:PRIMARY> cfg.members[2].hidden = true

true

s-1-rs:PRIMARY> rs.reconfig(cfg)

{ "ok" : 1 }
```

2. Check the replica set configuration again, member id=2 has "hidden" property set to true.

```
PRIMARY> cfg.members[2].priority = 0

{

        "_id" : 2,

        "host" : "n2.mongo.com:27017",

        "arbiterOnly" : false,

        "buildIndexes" : true,

        "hidden" : true,

        "priority" : 0,

        "tags" : {


        },
```

```
                    "slaveDelay" : 0,

                    "votes" : 1

              }

        ],

        "settings" : {

              "chainingAllowed" : true,

              "heartbeatTimeoutSecs" : 10,

              "getLastErrorModes" : {

              },

              "getLastErrorDefaults" : {

                    "w" : 1,

                    "wtimeout" : 0

              }
```

There is another special hidden member that stores a historical snapshot of primary data set, its appropriately called delayed replica set members.

Delayed Replica Set Members.

Delayed replica set members are another sub classification of a Hidden members. Like other secondary members , these also store copies of primary member and vote in elections.

Unlike other members that are kept as close to primary as possible, delayed replica set members have data set that reflect historical snapshot of primary dataset .

This delay is intentional to help recover data from unsuccessful upgrades or restore in case of human errors like inadvertent database or collection dropped.

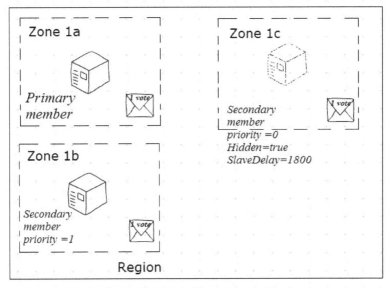

Delayed replica set member

Figure

4.5

We will add a delay of 30 minutes to our member with member id=2

```
s-1-rs:PRIMARY> cfg.members[2].slaveDelay = 1800

1800

{

                "_id" : 2,

                "host" : "n2.mongo.com:27017",

                "arbiterOnly" : false,

                "buildIndexes" : true,

                "hidden" : true,

                "priority" : 0,

                "tags" : {


                },

                "slaveDelay" : 1800,

                "votes" : 1

        }

    ],
```

To recap we have a member that can't be a primary, is hidden from client applications and has a replication lag of 30 minutes.

Since we need it in the next section to understand role of arbiter, lets revert the member back to where it was (as a full-fledged secondary member, with priority 1).

```
s-1-rs:PRIMARY> cfg.members[2].priority = 1

1

s-1-rs:PRIMARY> cfg.members[2].hidden = false

false

s-1-rs:PRIMARY> cfg.members[2].slaveDelay = 0

0

s-1-rs:PRIMARY> rs.reconfig(cfg)

{ "ok" : 1 }
```

Replica set with arbiter

An arbiter is a special secondary replica set member (*figure 4.6*). This member acts as referee and does not participate in any data activity in the cluster.

- o Arbiter does not have a copy of data set and hence cannot become a primary.
- o If you have even number of members in replica set, add an arbiter to add the deciding vote without necessity to having to store data and other related overheads.

o For obvious reasons adding an arbiter is beneficial if number of members in replica set is even, adding it to replica set with odd number of members may result in tied election.

o There is no data exchange to and from arbiters, the only communication between arbiters and other set members are votes during elections, heartbeats, and configuration data.

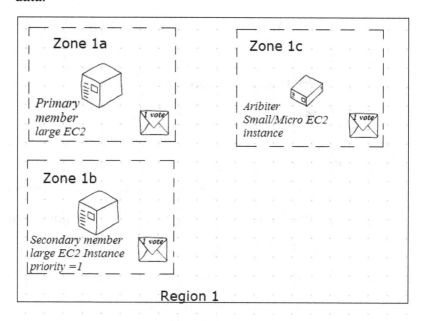

Arbiter in Replica set

Figure 4.6

Here we will try to take down a secondary member and will make it an Arbiter that can only elect primary. If you ever have to do this at your site, there are two ways this can be accomplished.

- o You can either reuse the Port,or you may operate the arbiter on the same port as the former secondary. For this to happen you must shut down the secondary and remove its data before restarting and reconfiguring it as an arbiter. Or

- o Start arbiter on a new port.

Here is how our Replica set looks like, right now *n1.mongo.com* is a secondary member. We will convert this node from a priority 1 secondary member to arbiter

	Name	Instance ID	Instance Type	Availability Zone
■	n1.mongo.com	i-4c2370b3	m3.medium	us-east-1a
■	n2.mongo.com	i-529013fb	m3.medium	us-east-1c
■	n3.mongo.com	i-87d5ff57	m3.medium	us-east-1d
■	NAT Instance (Public Subnet)	i-223e6ddd	t2.small	us-east-1a

1. Go to AWS console home and stop *n1.mongo.com*

MongoDB on AWS

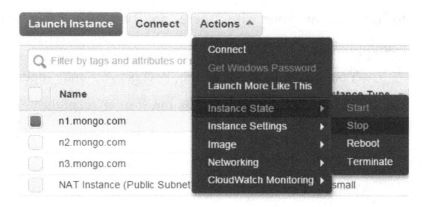

2. We will remove the member from replica set to convert it to arbiter

```
s-1-rs:PRIMARY> rs.remove("n1.mongo.com:27017")

{ "ok" : 1 }
```

3. Check the configuration of the replica set , you should see only 2 members

```
s-1-rs:PRIMARY> rs.conf()

{

    "_id" : "s-1-rs",

    "version" : 16,

    "members" : [

        {
```

MongoDB Cluster-Replica set

```
            "_id" : 1,

            "host" : "n3.mongo.com:27017",

            "arbiterOnly" : false,

            "buildIndexes" : true,

            "hidden" : false,

            "priority" : 1,

            "tags" : {

            },

            "slaveDelay" : 0,

            "votes" : 1

        },

        {

            "_id" : 2,

            "host" : "n2.mongo.com:27017",

            "arbiterOnly" : false,

            "buildIndexes" : true,

            "hidden" : false,

            "priority" : 1,

            "tags" : {

            },

            "slaveDelay" : 0,

            "votes" : 1
```

MongoDB Cluster-Replica set

```
            }
        ],
        "settings" : {
            "chainingAllowed" : true,
            "heartbeatTimeoutSecs" : 10,
            "getLastErrorModes" : {
            },
            "getLastErrorDefaults" : {
                "w" : 1,
                "wtimeout" : 0
            }
        }
    }
```

4. Since we are converting the instance *n1.mongo.com* to arbiter ,
   we don't need to use *m3.medium* family . let's change the
   instance type to something that's more economical and suitable
   for its status.

5. Choose the new instance type as *t2.small*, you can choose any instance as long as its 64 bit Linux system.

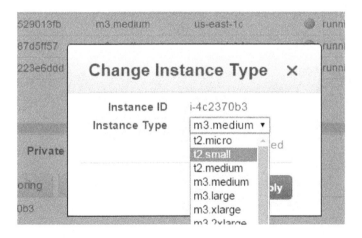

6. Start the instance once again and ssh into the new instance.
7. We need to empty the data directory for *n1.mongo.com* instance next, stop the mongod daemon

```
[ec2-user@n1.mongo.com mongo]$ sudo service mongod stop

Stopping mongod:                              [ OK  ]
```

8. Move the contents of data directory into an archive folder.

```
sudo mv /var/lib/mongo /var/lib/mongo_arch
```

9. Create an empty data directory

```
[ec2-user@n1.mongo.com mongo]$ sudo mkdir /var/lib/mongo

[ec2-user@n1.mongo.com mongo]$ cd /var/lib/mongo

[ec2-user@n1.mongo.com mongo]$ ls

[ec2-user@n1.mongo.com mongo]$
```

10. Change the group and owner to be mongod for the new directory

```
sudo chown mongod:mongod /var/lib/mongo
```

11. Start the mongod on the instance using a new port

```
[root@n1.mongo.com ~]# mongod --port 27061 --dbpath /var/lib/mongo --
replSet s-1-rs --smallfiles
```

2015-06-11T13:58:44.475+0000 I JOURNAL [initandlisten] journal dir=/var/lib/mongo/journal

2015-06-11T13:58:44.475+0000 I JOURNAL [initandlisten] recover : no journal files present, no recovery needed

2015-06-11T13:58:44.482+0000 I JOURNAL [durability] Durability thread started

2015-06-11T13:58:44.483+0000 I JOURNAL [journal writer] Journal writer thread started

2015-06-11T13:58:44.485+0000 I CONTROL [initandlisten] MongoDB starting : pid=3240 port=27061 dbpath=/var/lib/mongo 64-bit host=n1.mongo.com

2015-06-11T13:58:44.485+0000 I CONTROL [initandlisten] ** WARNING: You are running this process as the root user, which is not recommended.

2015-06-11T13:58:44.485+0000 I CONTROL [initandlisten]

2015-06-11T13:58:44.485+0000 I CONTROL [initandlisten]

2015-06-11T13:58:44.485+0000 I CONTROL [initandlisten] ** WARNING: /sys/kernel/mm/transparent_hugepage/defrag is 'always'.

2015-06-11T13:58:44.485+0000 I CONTROL [initandlisten] **   We suggest setting it to 'never'

2015-06-11T13:58:44.485+0000 I CONTROL [initandlisten]

2015-06-11T13:58:44.485+0000 I CONTROL [initandlisten] db version v3.0.3

```
2015-06-11T13:58:44.485+0000 I CONTROL  [initandlisten] git version:
b40106b36eecd1b4407eb1ad1af6bc60593c6105

2015-06-11T13:58:44.485+0000 I CONTROL  [initandlisten] OpenSSL
version: OpenSSL 1.0.0-fips 29 Mar 2010

2015-06-11T13:58:44.486+0000 I CONTROL  [initandlisten] build info:
Linux ip-10-30-227-48 3.4.43-43.43.amzn1.x86_64 #1 SMP Mon May 6
18:04:41 UTC 2013 x86_64 BOOST_LIB_VERSION=1_49

2015-06-11T13:58:44.486+0000 I CONTROL  [initandlisten] allocator:
tcmalloc

2015-06-11T13:58:44.486+0000 I CONTROL  [initandlisten] options: {
net: { port: 27061 }, replication: { replSet: "s-1-rs" }, storage: { dbPath:
"/var/lib/mongo", mmapv1: { smallFiles: true } } }

2015-06-11T13:58:44.489+0000 I REPL    [initandlisten] Did not find local
replica set configuration document at startup;  NoMatchingDocument Did
not find replica set configuration document in local.system.replset

2015-06-11T13:58:44.489+0000 I NETWORK  [initandlisten] waiting for
connections on port 27061
```

12. Start the mongo shell on the primary and using *rs.addArb*
    command add the new *t1.micro* instance as an arbiter

```
s-1-rs:PRIMARY> rs.addArb("n1.mongo.com:27061")

{ "ok" : 1 }
```

13. Check the replica set configuration , you should see the *arbiterOnly* property for the instance set to true

```
s-1-rs:PRIMARY> rs.conf()

    {

                "_id" : 3,

                "host" : "n1.mongo.com:27061",

                "arbiterOnly" : true,

                "buildIndexes" : true,

                "hidden" : false,

                "priority" : 1,

                "tags" : {

                },

                "slaveDelay" : 0,

                "votes" : 1

        }
```

Read semantics

We can redirect the read traffic going to replica set to any instance of your choice. If latency is an issue and we want client application to read the data from nearest deployed instance, it's possible to do that in *MongoDB*.

By default, an application reads data from the primary member in a replica set. Since writes are always directed to primary this approach has intrinsic benefit of reading latest data from the primary member .For an applications/Client where near real-time read is not a necessity, read throughput can be increased by routing some or all reads to secondary members of the replica set.

Read preference modes

Primary: Default mode .all read operations use only the current replica set primary. If the primary is unavailable, read operations throw an exception.

Primary preferred: Primary is given preference during read operations, if the primary is unavailable during failover situations, operations read from secondary members. Data "freshness" is not guaranteed and when primary member is not available, read operations may return stale data in some situations.

Secondary: Read only from the secondary members of the set. If no secondary's are available read operation produces an error or exception. Read operations using the secondary mode may more often than not return stale data.

secondary Preferred: secondary members are preferred during reads, the read operation will use the primary if no secondary is available (ex: in a standalone MongoDB install).

MongoDB Cluster-Replica set

Nearest: Members type is not taken into account, its proximity is the deciding factor (*figure 4.7*). Reads are routed to nearest member of the set according to the member selection process. Set this mode to minimize the effect of network latency on read operations without preference for current or stale data. If you are deploying the *MongoDB* instances across regions based on ping distance reads may be routed to the nearest region.

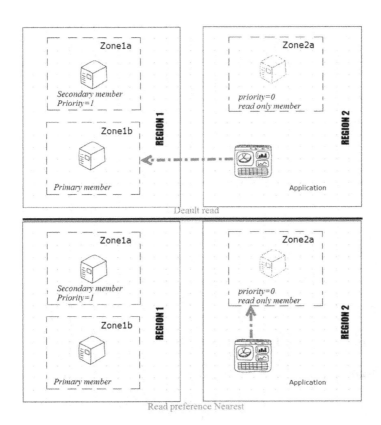

MongoDB Cluster-Replica set

To set the read preference mode , connect to mongo shell and execute the method *setReadPref*

```
db.getMongo().setReadPref('<mode>')
```

Where   mode   can   be   primary,   primaryPreferred
, secondary, secondaryPreferred, or nearest.

Replication backstage tour

Data synchronization during replication

During replication the secondary members replicate data from the primary. This operation of data sync comes in two flavors.

Initial Sync: This sync occurs when MongoDB creates or restores a member.

Continual Sync /Replication: occurs continually to keep the member updated with changes to the replica set's data.

Initial Sync

Initial sync copies all the data from one member of the replica set to another member. A member uses initial sync when the member has no data, such as when the member is initialized, or member recovered from an outage and may not have all the historical data.

During initial sync following activities are performed by Mongod

Clones all databases- mongod queries every collection in each source database and inserts all valid data into copies of these collections it maintains. During cloning _id indexes are also built. When the clone process omits an invalid document from the sync, MongoDB writes a message to the logs that begins with Cloner: found corrupt document in<collection>.

Applies all changes – Mongod using the oplog from the source applied the changes to the data set, the mongod updates its data set to reflect the current state of the replica set.

Builds indexes- Mongod builds indexes on all collections. Only exception are _id indexes which are built during cloning activity.

After mongod finishes building all indices, the member can transition to a normal state of being a secondary member.

Following activities are performed by admins to do a resync of secondary members

Restart with empty data –to do a resync either restart the mongod with an empty data directory and let *MongoDB's* normal initial syncing feature restore the data. This is the simple option time consuming in terms of when data sync gets complete.

Restart with copied data- In this procedure admins restart the machine with a copy of a recent data directory from another member in the replica set. This requires more manual steps but is quicker than restarting with empty data.

Continual sync

When we setup a replica set and designate members to it, replica set members replicate data continuously after the initial sync. This is an ongoing process that keeps the members caught-up with all changes to the replica set's data. default in continual sync secondary members synchronize from the primary but depending on ping times and the state of other members replication secondary members may change their sync targets if needed .

Replication lag

One reason there may be issues to elect a suitable primary is excessive replication Lag between primary and secondary members, it can also make distributed reads inconsistent. Replication lag is a delay between an operation on the primary and the infusion of that operation from the oplog to the secondary. Replication lag can be a significant issue and can seriously affect MongoDB replica set deployments.

Usual suspects of replication lag include

Network Latency

Ping the network routes between the replica set members to make sure there is no packet loss or network routing issue. Use traceroute to expose the routing of packets network endpoints.

Disk Throughput

Disk related issues can be transient with Amazon's EBS system. Disk throughput can be an issue if the file system and disk device on the secondary is unable to flush data to disk as quickly as the primary, making it difficult for secondary to keep in sync. This can be an issue in virtualized instances. Use system-level tools like iostat and *vmstat* to assess disk status.

Concurrency

When your primary is busy during peak workload windows, long-running operations on the primary can block replication on secondaries. When volume of write operations increase due to peak bulk operations, secondary members may have difficulty applying the replicating operations from the primary at a sufficient rate to keep them in sync. It is recommended to configure write concern to require confirmation of replication to secondaries. Specify a write concern with each write operation and include a timeout threshold for a write concern. This prevents write operations from returning if replication cannot keep up with the write load.

The following sequence of commands makes sure that majority of voting members receive the write operation before returning for next write operation.

```
s-1-rs:PRIMARY> rs.conf()

cfg = rs.conf()

cfg.settings = {}

cfg.settings.getLastErrorDefaults = { w: "majority", wtimeout: 5000 }

rs.reconfig(cfg)
```

Appropriate Write Concern

During bulk load operation in peak workloads the secondaries will not be able to read the oplog fast enough to keep up with changes.

Configure write acknowledgment or journaled write concern after fixed interval to provide an opportunity for secondaries to sync up with the primary oplog. Acknowledged write concern also allow clients to catch network, duplicate key, and other errors. During journaled write concern *MongoDB* acknowledges the write operation only after committing the data to the journal. This functionality also allows MongoDB to recover the data following an abnormal interruption.

To check the current length of replication lag ,connect to mongo shell connected to the primary, call the *rs.printSlaveReplicationInfo()* method This method returns the *syncedTo* value for each member, *syncedTo* is the time when the last oplog entry was passed to the secondary.

Please refer *MongoDB* documentation for more information on write concern in case of replica sets.

http://docs.mongodb.org/manual/core/write-concern/#replica-set-write-concern

Elections to select Primary member

Just like elections in real world, a server (in AWS terminology an instance) needs majority to be elected as a Primary. As we saw earlier, primary is chosen by replica set and is not a fixed instance (though there are ways to rig the process and chose your desired candidate as Primary).In the example we just saw with 3 member replica set every few seconds each server sends a heartbeat signal to every other member. Each member that is eligible to become primary (priority 1 members) stores these received messages in internal replicas set map. This map is a personal log book of the member that keeps them informed of what's happening around them. Any significant activity of a member becoming inactive/unreachable or state changes, ping distance of the member etc is logged in the map.

We create a replica set with three members. Why three why not two members one secondary and another primary. Well that's called a master slave configuration and is not suited for automatic failover. In a two member replica set if primary goes down secondary has no other members voting for it hence primary never gets elected and the whole reason to have a replica set (to do automatic failover) is defeated. We created an arbiter to resolve issues like these (an even number of replica set members)

When primary member goes down

When a replica set Primary goes down following election activity takes place at each secondary member

Self-appraisal: Each member looks for primary eligibility , does it qualify for election (priority 0 , Hidden and arbiter members fail this test).

Candidacy broadcast: If the member is eligible it sends out a message to other set members about its intention of becoming primary. There are frantic sanity checks at the other members and if all other member has a lower priority or less recent data the answer is affirmative. The secondary member is now an election candidate.

Election: Once the eligible secondary member gets the green signal from remaining alive members of replica set, its sends a "formal" message to all the members. The members do one quick sanity check and lock their votes for the candidate. The votes are locked for 30 seconds and if no other member veto's the member announcing candidacy is announced the new primary.

When secondary member goes down

When a secondary member goes down, following activities takes place in background.

Confidence vote: Primary member will send out message to other members of replica set to make sure it can reach majority and is still eligible for a primary

Stepping down: Primary steps down if it's unable to get ping from majority members. Primary closes all client connections before stepping down. If client applications use safe writes they will get socket error for the next write message fired towards the Primary member. When the primary member steps down and new primary is chosen any operations applied on the old primary are rolled back. The old primary joins the replica set as a secondary member and tries to sync itself with new Primary member.

We can also force a primary member to go down, say for maintenance or because we want to upgrade the instance family from *m3.medium* to *m3.large*. To force a primary to step down use *rs.stepDown ()* method

Replica-set deployment considerations

Same region -multiple Availability Zones

The templated deployments we carried out were all in the same region (*figure 4.8*). Deploying a replica set in a single region across availability zones ensures continuity to the cluster if one availability zone goes down. Availability zone in a region are isolated locations , connection to each other via low latency links.

MongoDB Cluster-Replica set

MongoDB on AWS

Figure 4.8

The regions on the other hand are completely independent.

Deploying *MongoDB* instances across availability zones provide redundancy and continuity, even if one zone goes down database is operational. Since the links between zones are low latency replication lag due to network is minimal.

When we create amazon VPC spanning multiple zones in the same region (*figure 4.9*), the MongoDB subnet needs to be in the same zone as it cannot span availability zones.to give uniformity to the communication from instances create a security group that's common to all subnets

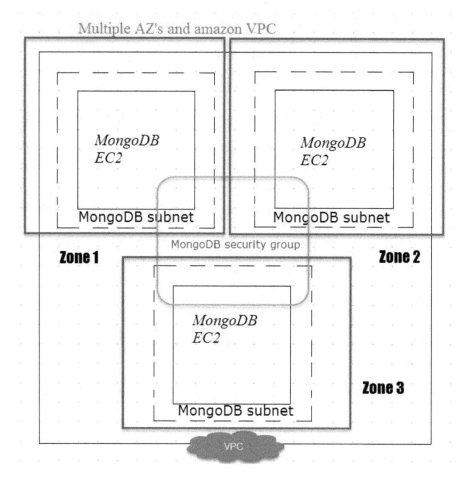

Figure 4.9

Choosing a single region also makes sense if the consumer applications all lie in the vicinity of same region. Example if the client applications using mongoDB all lie in US east coast, it makes little sense to deploy any instance in any of the Asia pacific regions.

Multiple regions- multiple availability Zones

MongoDB Cluster-Replica set

Deploying MongoDB replica set across regions gives more redundancy and availability, you can manipulate the elections to make sure the instance in your desired region is chosen as primary .

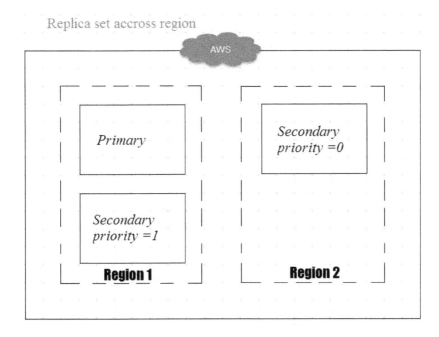

Figure 4.10

For a three member replica set we can deploy a primary and secondary in region 1 both with priority 1 and another secondary in region 2 with priority 0. This way when primary in region goes down the secondary in the same region becomes the new primary (*figure 4.10*).

The secondary in the region 2 can be leveraged to process the read request by application closest to it, by setting read preference nearest.

When deploying across regions please remember the regions are isolated locations with communication happening over internet. Apart from latency involved with such an arrangement you cannot use private IP's to communicate between EC2 in separate regions. When you set up virtual private cloud you get complete control over your virtual network, the VPC cannot span a region unless you create VPN.

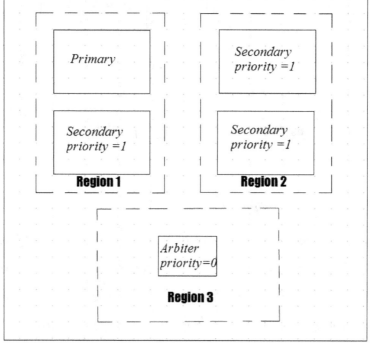

Figure 4.11

To control communications between instances in different regions use

IPtables on Linux to restrict traffic only to certain IP addresses and ports.

Another replica set configuration that tolerates network partitions and region fault tolerance is to deploy equal number of EC2 instances in separate regions and deploying arbiter in the third region (*figure 4.11*).

If a network partition disconnects region 1 and primary is unreachable arbiter (region3) and both secondary nodes can still complete quorum to go through an election to choose a new primary (*figure 4.12*).

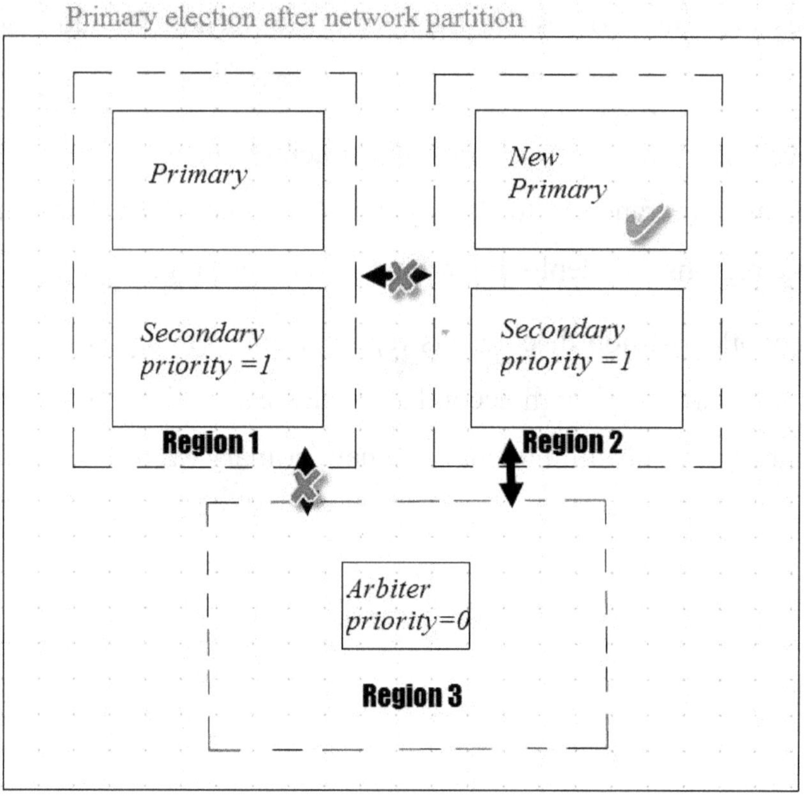

Primary election after network partition

Figure 4.12

When deploying *MongoDB* across regions create an amazon VPC in each region and control port security with security groups. Create multiple security groups for traffic flowing inside and outside the region.

You can also secure the communication between different regions by using secure IPsec tunnels or using SSL encryption and allowing EC2 instances to communicate with public IP addresses.

Chapter 5

Horizontal Scaling – Sharding

Chapter Objectives

> ➢ *Horizontal scaling using mongoDB shards.*

> ➢ *Sharding components, balancer and chunk migration.*

> ➢ *Shard key and selection criteria.*

> ➢ *Deploying a sharded cluster using MMS.*

> ➢ *Location aware sharding and sharding under the hood.*

> ➢ *Deploying sharded cluster across AWS availability zones and regions.*

....

I f you are running a *MongoDB* setup on AWS, as your data traffic increases you might start noticing one or all of the following events in your cluster.

- *Your disk space for data directory keeps getting full*

- *Client applications are screaming about the slow I/O throughput out of mongoDB.*

- *There is increasing page faults and servers are busy in paging more often than doing the actual data processing. i.e. RAM is becoming a bottleneck.*

Most often these issues point towards insufficient server capacity, there are two ways we can increase the performance of a *MongoDB* node (EC2 Instance). One way is to scale vertically by adding more RAM/CPU by using a bigger instance (for ex: move from *m3.medium* to *m3.large*).

Alternate way is to scale horizontally, by distributing the workload to more nodes. What we did with replica sets was increasing the redundancy of data , thus making our ensemble highly available. We indirectly diverted some read operations from data hotspots towards secondary instances to ease bottlenecks on primary, but it did not "explicitly" increase the performance of your write operations.

With sharding we are using a set of medium size machines, than partitioning the data into multiple chunks and storing subset of data in each machine (or EC2 instance).

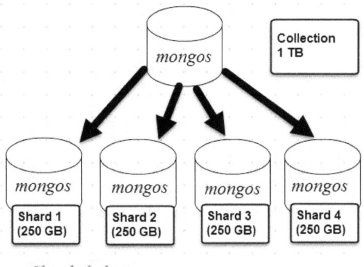

Sharded cluster

Figure 5.1

In MongoDB terms these cluster of machines on which data subsets are stored are called shards. A sharded cluster has no limitation on number of machines you can shard on , multiple shards should look like a single database to the client application. When we insert or read the collection *MongoDB* processes takes care of routing the request to different shards. The client application still interacts with *MongoDB* the way they interact with an unsharded cluster. What and how this routing takes place is invisible to the client applications.

Sharding components

Mongos-Tracing the steps from client application to data, mongos are the client interface for *MongoDB*. *Mongos* is the routing service for sharding that refers a data directory for locating actual position of data . Whenever a request reaches router it refers the data directory to fetch the correct information (read) or route the data to its destination (write).For a client application nothing changes, they feel they are interacting with a single mongod.

mongos usually run on appservers and do not store any data ,there can be multiple mongos in a cluster to divide the I/O request from sharded cluster (*figure 5.2*).

Config-servers- *config-servers* are book-keepers, they store the metadata for cluster. Since they store configuration details of the sharded cluster they are appropriately named *config-server*. *Config-server's* metadata provide the logical link between shards and data, without them *mongos* will be lost. They are also responsible for keeping the cluster balanced by doing data migrations if need arises (we will look at the examples later in this chapter) .We can say they are most critical piece of a sharded cluster. *config-servers* are lightweight processes and do not need a specific hardware configuration, they can run on any server.

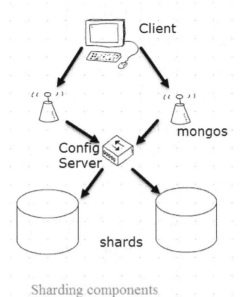

Sharding components

Figure 5.2

Since config servers are the brains behind sharding, it's a common practice to have more than one *config-server* for cluster fault tolerance.

When mongos start the first time they cache the metadata from config servers for faster retrieval each time a read/write comes to it.

Shards-shards are containers where actual data is stored.

Data distribution and chunk migration

Shard key is the single biggest design investment when it comes to

MongoDB sharding. Choosing a bad shard key will keep your cluster busy balancing itself or break your application when traffic is at the heaviest and you need the cluster up and running.

A key difference between horizontal partitioning accomplished in most other databases and *MongoDB* is automatic balancing in *MongoDB*. A bad shard key is sure way of killing your system by overloading certain shards or creating data "hot spots".

A good shard key will be a boon as *MongoDB* will balance the cluster automatically ,whenever more data or servers are added to the cluster.

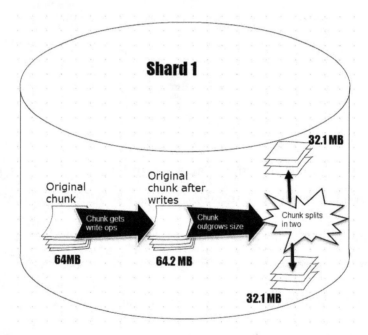

Horizontal Scaling – Sharding

Figure 5.3

MongoDB stores data in shards in 64MB (by default) contiguous spaces called chunks .The chunk size is configurable but we will look in the chapter why it's not a good idea to play with the chunk size (unless you are doing it intentionally and prepared for ramifications).

Sharding in *MongoDB* achieves "Auto balancing" for the cluster, provided choice of shard key is ideal .*MongoDB* will keep the cluster healthy and balanced by executing following actions

As soon as data in shard grows more than what the chunk can accommodate, the chunk splits (figure 5.3).

And

When a shard contains too many chunks compared to other shards data migration happens.

A chunk in a shard contains is a range of data, To understand it with an example let's take the following collection. This contains telephone number area codes, name and age of corresponding subscriber.

{"Name" : "Sherry", "Area Code" : 123 , "age" :32}

{"Name" : "matthew", " Area Code" : 113 , "age" :25}

{"Name" : "Jay", " Area Code" : 263 , "age" :63}

{"Name" : "Ben", " Area Code" : 235 , "age" :63}

{"Name" : "Berry", " Area Code" : 415 , "age" :17}

{"Name" : "Robert", " Area Code" : 312, "age" :77}

{"Name" : "sumit", " Area Code" : 527, "age" :46}

If we choose "area code" as the shard key ,to co-locate area codes together. The chunk [100 to 300) 4will contain the following documents

{"Name" : "Sherry", "Area Code" : 123 , "age" :32}

{"Name" : "matthew", " Area Code" : 113 , "age" :25}

{"Name" : "Jay", " Area Code" : 263 , "age" :63}

{"Name" : "Ben", " Area Code" : 235 , "age" :63}

If there are more numbers in this range and the size of this chunk exceeds 64MB, the chunk will split in the middle. Two new chunks thus created would be [100 to 200) and [200 to 300)

New distribution would be

Chunk [100 to 200)

{"Name" : "Sherry", "Area Code" : 123 , "age" :32}

---

[4] Mathematical set notation is used here, '[' and ']' signify the set includes the number .'('means number greater than and excluding the number , '(' denotes less than and not including the number.

{"Name" : "matthew", " Area Code" : 113 , "age" :25}

Chunk [200 to 300)

{"Name" : "Jay", " Area Code" : 263 , "age" :63}

{"Name" : "Ben", " Area Code" : 235 , "age" :63}

When you start your cluster it starts with a single shard (Shard 1) as your data grows you add another shard mongoDB will look at the chunks and try to move data to the new shard so that the cluster is balanced.

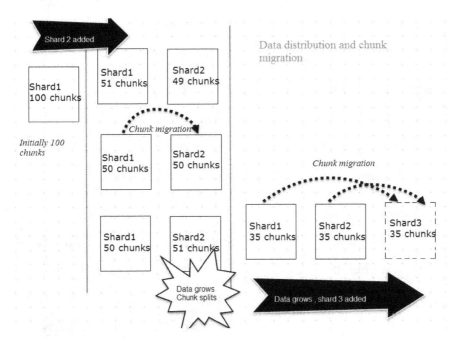

Horizontal Scaling – Sharding

Figure 5.4

As the cluster becomes imbalanced chunks move to and from till your physical disk space becomes a bottleneck.

To scale horizontally more shards are added and chunks migrate to rebalance the cluster. Sharding makes *MongoDB* cluster a thriving breathing system (*figure 5.4*).

As discussed earlier mongos store metadata in its cache for faster retrieval of information during read writes. *mongos* refresh the cache each time they restart to look for any changes in metadata. The cache refresh also happens after each chunk migration. Chunk migration changes the data location and metadata in *config-servers*.

MongoDB distributes data automatically but data movement is never a good thing if it's just to keep the cluster balanced. The process that rebalances the cluster is known as balancer and it's written in a way to avoid unnecessary chunk migrations.

For a balancer to take charge there should be at-least 9 more chunks than the least populated shard for the chunk to migrate from one shard to another. The balancer should not be constantly busy in balancing the cluster , to avoid that never create smaller chunk . small chunk size will fill up quickly and will tilt the balance more often than necessary.

Keeping the default chunk size (64MB) , we would need at least 2 GB

(9 chunks * 64 MB) worth of data size difference between shards to trigger data movement between them.

2 GB is good amount of data that's why 64 MB chunk size hits the sweet spot and works for most databases, and may work for your setup too.

Shard key selection

From an application design perspective, sharding is all about choosing the right shard key. During a read operation *mongos* will route queries to a shard or subset of shards only when a shard key is used in the query. If shard key is not used there is no way for mongos to identify where data is located it's going to hit all over the place and broadcast the query to all shards. Also remember documents having the same value for the shard key will be located on the same shard.

For starting sharding on a collection, an Index should exist on the shard key. For an Empty collection if *MongoDB* will put an index on the shard key automatically. For an existing collection you are planning to shard later, Index needs to be defined explicitly on the shard key.

For reading data we would like to filter as much as we can and go to as fewer disk locations as possible. In other words we want our queries to be qualified and to save seek time data elements to be located within close proximity (or in a single shard). For writing we need almost opposite to be true, data should be distributed so that operations can

Horizontal Scaling – Sharding

write data to multiple shards in parallel thus enhancing the write throughput.

So we have two mutually exclusive objectives but one method (sharding) to achieve both results. How to go about our design to choose a key that gives optimal performance in read/writes with sharded cluster. First question we need to ask ourselves is what takes precedence in the priority list, read performance or write throughput. Once you have answered this basic question, following are some important criteria to keep in mind for shard key selection.

> ***Choose keys with high cardinality***: cardinality refers to distinct values of an attribute. To understand issue with choosing a sharding key with low cardinality (or less unique values) , consider a collection consisting of 50 US states. Assuming the application designers used state as the shard key, the choice looks appropriate in the beginning as most queries will be covered by a particular state hence you are hitting only a single shard for reading and writing.

> Initially when data volume is manageable, all the data will reside in a single shard. Over a period of time the data grows we add a new shard and the data is evenly distributed.

Let's assume with passage of time we get disproportionately more data for California , we cannot spread the chunks to different shards for shard key California if we do that shard key values for California would need to exist in two different shards . When a shard key with low cardinality is chosen the only scaling that can happen is vertical i.e. we need to add more disk space to the shard to accommodate shard with overwhelming data. A high cardinality shard key for ex Zip code can be easily spread across more shards.

Whatever shard key we choose should be able to spread easily to different shards. If shard key is not easily divisible, it will inhibit the chunk movement from one shard to another triggering a imbalanced cluster.

Shard key with low cardinality equates to low horizontal scaling, high cardinality shard key equates to high degree of horizontal scaling using shards.

Keys with monotonically increasing values: When there is temporal data (time series data), often it plays an important role on how documents are accessed from a collection. It's common to create shard key on a date/timestamp field. This approach is a sure shot way of creating data hotspots.

Ex: for a twitter feeds if we create the shard key on the timestamp when the twitter post was created. You will have more write activity to the shard that contains the most current data. Even if the chunk split and migration happens the recent data will always be together.

This principle of data hotspots hold true for any key with monotonically increasing values (i.e. not only time series data), the most recent data will almost certainly reside in a single shard. Unless you are sure that your shards will receive a limited traffic and is able to handle the volume, don't use ascending data values for shard key.

Random distribution – Another way to choose a shard key is to allow any random field be the shard key. Idea is since the key values are random they are most probably of high cardinality. To take the example of storing twitter posts we may choose the twitter handle as the shard key. This choice will get us the write scaling since with high cardinality comes a balanced distribution of data across the shards. There are two flaws with this approach first is you may be wasting an Index .Since the shard key needs an index on the shard key, if you will never use the field in your queries (remember you have chosen a key with random values) you are wasting an index. Secondly your query isolation will suffer, we didn't choose to co-locate data in shards based on their co-relation to each other. Since the distribution was based on random values, for data values searched together you will be searching all the shards.

To summarize ask these question when choosing shard key for your sharded cluster.

o Look for access patterns, how you access your data? What values you use together?

Ex: Is your queries always qualify the data based on Zip code or Dates?

o What is the frequency of your data writes? What is peak volume and when? How about reads, what the usage pattern with respect to time?

o When using a field for shard key , what will be the usage pattern are some value used more disproportionately than others

Ex: If using age as the shard key, are you getting more data for a particular age group?

A good shard key provides both high cardinality and even distribution of write operations across the shards.

Deploying a sharded cluster using MMS

In this section we will launch a sharded *MongoDB* cluster, we will be using *Mongodb Management Service* (MMS in short) to launch our cluster. MMS is a repeatable and easier way to do *MongoDB* deployments , similar to Cloud formation templates but custom built for MongoDB.

MongoDB management service

MongoDB management service (or MMS in short) is a service for managing mongoDB infrastructure. It simplify the following functions by providing them under one roof

o   Monitoring the hardware and database indicators and providing real-time statistics on health of your infrastructure.

o   Making configuration and provisioning activities for mongoDB deployments easier by automating them.

o   Scheduling point in time backup and snapshots of mongoDB databases.

To start using MMS , go to *cloud.mongodb.com* and signup for the service and build a new MongoDB deployment.

MongoDB on AWS

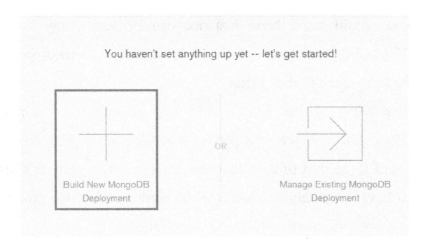

You haven't set anything up yet -- let's get started!

Build New MongoDB Deployment

OR

Manage Existing MongoDB Deployment

1. Click on deploy on AWS on the next screen.

2. On the next screen, allow cloud manager to provision the EC2 instance.

3. Create a sharded cluster

Standalone Instance

A standalone MongoDB provides a single copy of your data and is appropriate for projects where data loss is not a concern.

CREATE STANDALONE

Replica Set

A replica set is a group of MongoDB instances that host the same data set. A replica set provides both redundancy and high availability.

CREATE REPLICA SET

Sharded Cluster

Sharding is a method for storing data across multiple machines. MongoDB uses sharding to support deployments with very large data sets and high throughput operations.

CREATE SHARDED CLUSTER

4. Provide these details for your cluster

Cluster Name: Provide a cluster name

Shard Count: This relates to how many shard instances MMS will launch. Begin with 1 unless you already know how many

Horizontal Scaling – Sharding

you would need. New instance can be added any time and *MongoDB* takes care of balancing the cluster to incorporate the new instance in the cluster.

Nodes per shard: Each *shard* will be either a standalone *MongoDB* instance or a part of a replica set. If you want your shard to be part of a replica set , choose this option. It's alright to have a standalone shard for development, but for production at least 3 member replica set is recommended.

Number of servers: when we *shard* the document(s) we have a choice of keeping the shards in a single server or distribute it in another replicated primary. For the time being we will use a single replicated instance.

5. Before we can launch our cluster , access key to allow MMS to create the cluster on AWS would be needed.

6. Provide the AWS credentials to launch the credentials

7. In the EC2 configuration page, provide the instance type, Region, subnets and other details.

8. Before deploying you can view the mongoDB processes , *mongo-10-M3Large-us-east-1d* is the primary instance for the replica set we are launching ,with the 1 shard (shrd_0) that we provisioned.

9. The other two instances *mongo-12-M3Large-us-east-1a* and *mongo-11-M3 Large-us-east-1c* are secondary members of replica set.

To review once again we have launched a sharded cluster with single *Shard* , three *config servers* and a single *mongos*

10. Once deployed , we can view three mongoDB instances running on AWS

11. To connect to our Linux instances we would need private keys for ssh connections, from *cloud manager console* →*AWS settings* download private key on your desktop

12. If we navigate to ***/data*** directory in our instance we should see multiple directories for our shards, mongos and config server processes.

```
[ec2-user@mongo-10 data]$ cd /data
[ec2-user@mongo-10 data]$ ls
lost+found  prod-clstr1_config_38  prod-clstr1_mongos_41  prod-clstr1_shrd_0_35
```

If you open directories for each of the processes you will notice *mongos* does not store any namespace or bson storage files, while *config server* and *shard* do have these files. To reiterate *mongos* do not store any data and that's what we see on our recently launched EC2 instance.

13. To connect to your mongoDB cluster , click on the cluster name in the MMS console and click on

Connect to this instance

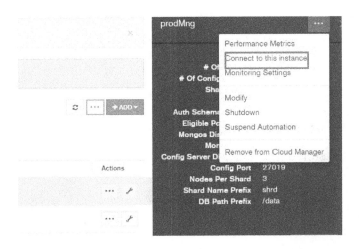

This will open another popup window with the required command to interact with your mongoDB cluster

MongoDB on AWS

Connect to Your Deployment

To connect to a Mongos in this Cluster via the mongo shell:

```
/var/lib/mongodb-mms-automation/mongodb-linux-x86_64-3.0.4/bin/mongo mongo-
.sumitmongodb.1659.mongodbdns.com:27017
```

Please note that you must connect from a server which is able to reach `mongo-6.sumitmongodb.1659.mongodbdns.com` on port `27017`. The path to the mongo shell (mongo) may be different if you connect from a different server.

Detailed information on connecting to your deployment is available here.

CLOSE

Open a new *ssh* connection on primary instance and test connecting to the *mongo* cluster.

```
[ec2-user@mongo-10 data]$ /var/lib/mongodb-mms-automation/mongodb-
linux-x86_64-3.0.4/bin/mongo mongo-
10.sumitmongodb.1659.mongodbdns.com:27000

MongoDB shell version: 3.0.4

connecting to: mongo-10.sumitmongodb.1659.mongodbdns.com:27000/test

Welcome to the MongoDB shell.

For interactive help, type "help".

For more comprehensive documentation, see

    http://docs.mongodb.org/
```

Questions? Try the support group

http://groups.google.com/group/mongodb-user

shrd_0:PRIMARY>

Checking the shard status: Connect to mongos on the primary and look for the shard status

```
[ec2-user@mongo-10 data]$ /var/lib/mongodb-mms-automation/mongodb-
linux-x86_64-3.0.4/bin/mongo mongo-
10.sumitmongodb.1659.mongodbdns.com:27017

MongoDB shell version: 3.0.4

connecting to: mongo-10.sumitmongodb.1659.mongodbdns.com:27017/test

mongos> use admin

switched to db admin

mongos> db.runCommand({listshards:1})
{
    "shards" : [
        {
            "_id" : "shrd_0",
            "host" : "shrd_0/mongo-
10.sumitmongodb.1659.mongodbdns.com:27000,
mongo-11.sumitmongodb.1659.mongodbdns.com:27000,
mongo-12.sumitmongodb.1659.mongodbdns.com:27000"
```

```
            }
        ],
        "ok" : 1
    }
mongos>
```

The ***db.runCommand({listshards:1})*** command lists the only shard shrd_0 that's running on the replica set, it also lists the replica set members where data would be replicated for this shard

14. We will change the chunk size of our cluster to 1 MB, we are doing this to showcase the chunk migration and balancer functionalities of cluster

```
shrd_0:PRIMARY> use config
switched to db config
shrd_0:PRIMARY> db.settings.save( { _id:"chunksize", value: 1 } )
WriteResult({ "nMatched" : 0, "nUpserted" : 1, "nModified" : 0, "_id" :
"chunksize" })
shrd_0:PRIMARY> db.settings.find()
{ "_id" : "chunksize", "value" : 1 }
```

Note: making chunksize 1 MB is a bad design choice, in fact the chunksize should not be touched unless you are absolutely certain what you need as chunksize. In any case 1 MB is too small value for any real world scenario.

15. Create a collection on *testdb* database named *BlogIDEntry* , this collection will contain the documents containing *blogid* and date of creation of the blog

```
shrd_0:PRIMARY> db.createCollection("BlogIDEntry", { capped : false,
autoIndexId : false } )
{ "ok" : 1 }
```

16. Connect to mongos and prepare the database *testdb* for sharding.

```
mongos> use admin
switched to db admin
mongos> db.runCommand({enablesharding:"testdb"})
{ "ok" : 1 }
```

17. Create a shard key on the empty collection , shard key would be on *blogid* field.

```
mongos>
db.runCommand({shardcollection:"testdb.BlogIDEntry",key:{blogid:1}})
```

```
{ "collectionsharded" : "testdb.BlogIDEntry", "ok" : 1 }
```

18. Let's add some sizable volume to the collection , we will add 5000000 documents to the collection

```
shrd_0:PRIMARY> for (i=0;i<=5000000;i++){db.BlogIDEntry.insert({"_id":
i,"created date":new Date(),"blogid":i});}
WriteResult({ "nInserted" : 1 })
shrd_0:PRIMARY> db.BlogIDEntry.count()
5000001
```

19. While you are inserting records check the shard distribution by connecting to the shard and executing
    db.BlogIDEntry.getShardDistribution()

```
[ec2-user@mongo-10 ~]$  /var/lib/mongodb-mms-automation/mongodb-linux-
x86_64-3.0.4/bin/mongo mongo-
10.sumitmongodb.1659.mongodbdns.com:27017

mongos> db.BlogIDEntry.getShardDistribution()
Shard shrd_0 at shrd_0/mongo-
10.sumitmongodb.1659.mongodbdns.com:27000,mongo-
11.sumitmongodb.1659.mongodbdns.com:27000,mongo-
12.sumitmongodb.1659.mongodbdns.com:27000

 data : 150.11MiB docs : 1405408 chunks : 1
```

estimated data per chunk : 150.11MiB

estimated docs per chunk : 1405408

Totals

data : 150.11MiB docs : 1405408 chunks : 1

Shard shrd_0 contains 100% data, 100% docs in cluster, avg obj size on shard : 112B

Adding a new shard using MMS

In this section we will add one more shard to our cluster, we will use MMS to add a shard.

    1. Click on cluster name →modify

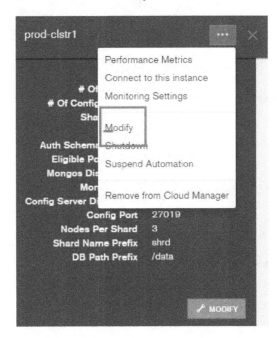

Horizontal Scaling – Sharding

2. On the shard configuration increase the shard count, we will increase the value from 1 to 2

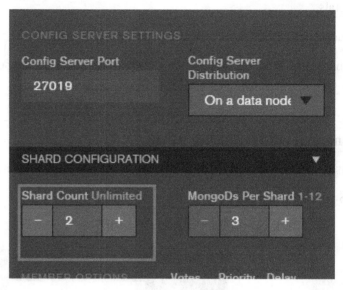

3. The changes won't take effect till they are reviewed and deployed

4. On the next window review changes

Review Your Changes

5. Login to primary instance again and view the contents of /data directory ,you should notice another subdirectory in this case its *prod-clstr1_shrd_1_42*

```
[ec2-user@mongo-10 data]$ ls -ltr

total 32

drwx------ 2 root   root   16384 Jun 27 11:56 lost+found

drwxr-xr-x 4 mongod mongod  4096 Jun 27 11:59 prod-clstr1_config_38

drwxr-xr-x 2 mongod mongod  4096 Jun 27 11:59 prod-clstr1_mongos_41

drwxr-xr-x 4 mongod mongod  4096 Jun 27 14:36 prod-clstr1_shrd_0_35

drwxr-xr-x 4 mongod mongod  4096 Jun 27 16:46 prod-clstr1_shrd_1_42
```

6. To check how many shards the cluster currently has , execute *db.runCommand({listshards:1})*

```
mongos> use admin
```

Horizontal Scaling – Sharding

```
switched to db admin

mongos> db.runCommand({listshards:1})

{

    "shards" : [

        {

            "_id" : "shrd_0",

            "host" : "shrd_0/mongo-
10.sumitmongodb.1659.mongodbdns.com:27000,mongo-
11.sumitmongodb.1659.mongodbdns.com:27000,mongo-
12.sumitmongodb.1659.mongodbdns.com:27000"

        },

        {

            "_id" : "shrd_1",

            "host" : "shrd_1/mongo-
10.sumitmongodb.1659.mongodbdns.com:27001,mongo-
11.sumitmongodb.1659.mongodbdns.com:27001,mongo-
12.sumitmongodb.1659.mongodbdns.com:27001"

        }

    ],

    "ok" : 1

}
```

Horizontal Scaling – Sharding

7. ***Sharding status :*** we can also do a health check on shards by executing *sh.status()* command

```
[ec2-user@mongo-10 ~]$  /var/lib/mongodb-mms-automation/mongodb-
linux-x86_64-3.0.4/bin/mongo mongo-
10.sumitmongodb.1659.mongodbdns.com:27017

MongoDB shell version: 3.0.4

connecting to: mongo-10.sumitmongodb.1659.mongodbdns.com:27017/test

mongos> sh.status()

--- Sharding Status ---

  sharding version: {

      "_id" : 1,

      "minCompatibleVersion" : 5,

      "currentVersion" : 6,

      "clusterId" : ObjectId("558e903ac012f3a8c7a0902b")

}

  shards:

      {  "_id" : "shrd_0", "host" :

"shrd_0/mongo-10.sumitmongodb.1659.mongodbdns.com:27000,

mongo-11.sumitmongodb.1659.mongodbdns.com:27000,

mongo-12.sumitmongodb.1659.mongodbdns.com:27000" }

      {  "_id" : "shrd_1", "host" :

"shrd_1/mongo-10.sumitmongodb.1659.mongodbdns.com:27001,
```

Horizontal Scaling – Sharding

mongo-11.sumitmongodb.1659.mongodbdns.com:27001,

mongo-12.sumitmongodb.1659.mongodbdns.com:27001" }

balancer:

    Currently enabled: yes

    Currently running: no

    Failed balancer rounds in last 5 attempts: 0

    Migration Results for the last 24 hours:

        No recent migrations

databases:

    { "_id" : "admin", "partitioned" : false, "primary" : "config" }

    { "_id" : "test", "partitioned" : false, "primary" : "shrd_0" }

    { "_id" : "testdb", "partitioned" : true, "primary" : "shrd_0" }

        testdb.BlogIDEntry

            shard key: { "blogid" : 1 }

            chunks:

                shrd_0 1

                { "blogid" : { "$minKey" : 1 } } -->> { "blogid" : { "$maxKey" : 1 } } on : shrd_0 Timestamp(1, 0)

8. if you insert some more volume (try inserting couple of million more documents) to the collection and query for

sharding status again, you would observe some interesting stats

```
mongos> sh.status()

     :

     :

  balancer:

     Currently enabled:  yes

     Currently running:  yes

            Balancer lock taken at Sat Jun 27 2015 20:33:15 GMT+0000
(UTC) by mongo-10:27017:1435406343:1804289383:Balancer:1681692777

     :

     :
```

Notice the difference in *sh.status()* output between last time to current iteration, the balancer was not running earlier, it was enabled though.

As there was another shard added and chunk imbalance increased between old and new shard balancer came into action and started moving chunks. This movement of chunks will not stop till the cluster is balanced. We would notice the chunks in shard_1 increasing with elapsing time.

Location aware sharding

Documents are partitioned according to a user-specified configuration that associates shard key ranges with shards hosted on specific physical instances. Administrators can control the location of data for application requirements such as placing data sets closest to its users, or regulatory controls determining where data can be physically stored. Location-aware sharding, also called *tag-aware* sharding, enables great flexibility in regional scaling. For example, a new service could experience explosive growth in Asia, requiring the addition of new shards just in that region. Administrators do not also have to add new shards in other regions as well.

Steps below outline the creation process for tag aware shards in our cluster.

1. To use tag based sharding we will be reusing the zips collection we used in previous chapters, if you don't have that in the new sharded cluster.

   Here are the quick steps to import it into our primary instance.

   Get the zips.json form media.mongodb.org (*http://media.mongodb.org/zips.json?_ga=1.88619867.1932956 186.1433008705*)

MongoDB on AWS

Change the directory to */var/lib/mongodb-mms-automation/mongodb-linux-x86_64-3.0.4/bin/* or wherever mongoimport utility is available in your install.

```
[ec2-user@mongo-10 ~]$ cd /var/lib/mongodb-mms-automation/mongodb-linux-x86_64-3.0.4/bin/
```

Use mongoimport to import the zips.json to censusdb database.

```
[ec2-user@mongo-10 bin]$ ./mongoimport --host mongo-10.sumitmongodb.1659.mongodbdns.com:27000 --db censusdb --collection statecensus  --file /home/ec2-user/zips.json
2015-06-28T12:36:38.172+0000    connected to: mongo-10.sumitmongodb.1659.mongodbdns.com:27000
2015-06-28T12:36:41.171+0000    [########..............] censusdb.zips    1.0 MB/3.0 MB (34.5%)
:

:

:
```

2. ***Enable sharding :*** Next step would be to enable sharding on ***censusdb*** database

```
mongos> sh.enableSharding('censusdb')
{ "ok" : 1 }
```

3. ***Create Index :*** Once *censusdb* is enabled to accept sharded collections, we will shard collection *zips* on state and zip field , for that we need to create an index on fields state and zip

```
mongos> db.statecensus.createIndex( { state:1,zip:1 } )
{
    "raw" : {
        "shrd_0/mongo-
10.sumitmongodb.1659.mongodbdns.com:27000,mongo-
11.sumitmongodb.1659.mongodbdns.com:27000,mongo-
12.sumitmongodb.1659.mongodbdns.com:27000" : {
                "createdCollectionAutomatically" : true,
                "numIndexesBefore" : 1,
                "numIndexesAfter" : 2,
                "ok" : 1,
                "$gleStats" : {
                    "lastOpTime" : Timestamp(1435504227, 2),
                    "electionId" : ObjectId("558e900b6b0c478786628db0")
                }
        }
}
```

```
    },
    "ok" : 1
}
```

While sharding the collection if we don't create an index on the shardkey we will get the error "errmsg" : *"please create an index that starts with the shard key before sharding."*

4. We can shard the collection on state field

```
mongos> sh.shardCollection('censusdb.statecensus', {state: 1,zip:1})
{ "collectionsharded" : "censusdb.statecensus", "ok" : 1 }
```

5. ***Adding shard tags :*** Add shard tags on the two running shards

```
mongos> use admin
switched to db admin
mongos> sh.addShardTag('shrd_0','East Coast')
mongos> sh.addShardTag('shrd_1','West Coast')
```

6. Running *sh.status* command will show how tags have been attached to the two shards existing shards

```
mongos> sh.status()
```

```
--- Sharding Status ---

  sharding version: {

      "_id" : 1,

      "minCompatibleVersion" : 5,

      "currentVersion" : 6,

      "clusterId" : ObjectId("558e903ac012f3a8c7a0902b")

}

  shards:

      { "_id" : "shrd_0", "host" :

"shrd_0/mongo-10.sumitmongodb.1659.mongodbdns.com:27000,

mongo-11.sumitmongodb.1659.mongodbdns.com:27000,

mongo-12.sumitmongodb.1659.mongodbdns.com:27000", "tags" : [ "East

Coast" ] }

      { "_id" : "shrd_1", "host" :

"shrd_1/mongo-10.sumitmongodb.1659.mongodbdns.com:27001,

mongo-11.sumitmongodb.1659.mongodbdns.com:27001,

mongo-12.sumitmongodb.1659.mongodbdns.com:27001", "tags" : [ "West

Coast" ] }
```

7. To check the chunk distribution we can use the config database and invoke *db.chunks.find*

We can see the chunk distribution, the number would depend on how many shards and the size of the chunk set for the cluster.

```
mongos> use config
switched to db config
mongos>
db.chunks.find({ns:"censusdb.statecensus"},{shard:1,_id:0}).sort({shard:1})
{ "shard" : "shrd_1" }
{ "shard" : "shrd_1" }
.......
```

8. Next step would be to move documents related to each individual state to relevant shard
   Ex:state MA to would be labeled with tag East Coast , East Coast is tagged to shard shard_0

```
mongos> sh.addTagRange( "censusdb.statecensus",{ state: "MA", zip: MinKey
},{ state: "MA", zip: MaxKey },"East Coast")
```

9. Upon invoking the *db.chunks.find* again you would find some chunks have migrated to shrd_0 from shrd_1. compare the *sh.status()* for summary before and after applying tags

```
Migration Results for the last 24 hours:
```

```
34 : Success

0 : Failed
```

Sharding under the hood

config server maintains a special database aptly named *config*. *config* database is internal database that mongoDB maintains for sharding purposes,we should never modify or query upon its content in the course of normal operation.

```
[ec2-user@mongo-10 ~]$ /var/lib/mongodb-mms-automation/mongodb-
linux-x86_64-3.0.4/bin/mongo mongo-
10.sumitmongodb.1659.mongodbdns.com:27017

MongoDB shell version: 3.0.4

connecting to: mongo-10.sumitmongodb.1659.mongodbdns.com:27017/test

mongos> use config

switched to db config

mongos> show collections

actionlog

changelog

chunks

collections

databases

lockpings
```

```
locks

mongos

settings

shards

system.indexes

tags

version

mongos>
```

o *config.versions* store the version of the current metadata, use *db.Collection* method to extract version number.

```
mongos> db.getCollection("version").find()
{ "_id" : 1, "minCompatibleVersion" : 5, "currentVersion" : 6, "clusterId" :
ObjectId("558e903ac012f3a8c7a0902b") }
```

o To look at collection list that have sharding enabled use the command *db.collections.find(). pretty()*

```
mongos> db.collections.find(). pretty()
{
    "_id" : "testdb.BlogIDEntry",
```

```
        "lastmod" : ISODate("2015-06-28T13:45:26.118Z"),

        "dropped" : true,

        "lastmodEpoch" : ObjectId("000000000000000000000000")

}
{

        "_id" : "censusdb.zips",

        "lastmod" : ISODate("2015-06-28T13:44:31.705Z"),

        "dropped" : true,

        "lastmodEpoch" : ObjectId("000000000000000000000000")

}
{

        "_id" : "censusdb.statecensus",

        "lastmod" : ISODate("2015-06-28T15:31:07.579Z"),

        "dropped" : false,

        "key" : {

            "state" : 1,

            "zip" : 1

        },

        "unique" : false,

        "lastmodEpoch" : ObjectId("5590133bc012f3a8c7a0b277")

}
```

Horizontal Scaling – Sharding

o The _id field gives the namespace of the collection in the < database >.< collection name > format, the key field gives the shard key, and the unique field indicates whether the shard key is unique of not. These three fields come as the three parameters of the *sh.shardCollection* function in that very order.

o To see if the balancer is enabled in your cluster, issue the *sh.getBalancerState()* command, which returns a boolean True or False value.

```
mongos> sh.getBalancerState()
true
```

o To see if the balancer process is active in your cluster, use *db.locks.find({ _id : "balancer" }).pretty()*

```
mongos> db.locks.find( { _id : "balancer" } ).pretty()
{
    "_id" : "balancer",
    "state" : 0,
```

```
        "who" : "mongo-
10:27017:1435925223:1804289383:Balancer:846930886",

        "ts" : ObjectId("5596b44715b9f03e28133c3e"),

        "process" : "mongo-10:27017:1435925223:1804289383",

        "when" : ISODate("2015-07-03T16:11:51.332Z"),

        "why" : "doing balance round"

    }
```

This output confirms that the balancer originates from the mongos running on the system with the hostname mongo-10.

The value in the state field indicates that a mongos has the lock the value of an active lock is 0.

To schedule the balancing window of the balancer, i.e to schedule the process so that balancer is active only at certain times. Use the *db.settings.update* method, and specify a time window when balancer would be active .

Before schedule can be assigned make sure balancer is in running state by using *setBalancerState()* method.

```
mongos> sh.getBalancerState(true)

true
```

Next use *db.setting.update()* method to schedule balancer to trigger during specified time window.

```
mongos> db.settings.update(

... { _id: "balancer" },

... { $set: { activeWindow : { start : "02:00", stop : "04:00" } } },

... { upsert: true }

... )

WriteResult({ "nMatched" : 0, "nUpserted" : 1, "nModified" : 0, "_id" :
"balancer" })
```

During what scenarios would we want to attach balancer schedule? balancer triggers chunk migrations and it can impact the performance of running cluster. We may want to do the balancing during off hours or in case you data grow slowly and may not need continual balancing of the cluster.

In case you are interested there are some interesting open source code on **github** to do a cluster health check, refer one of them below

https://github.com/serverdensity/mongodb-balance-check

Sharding deployment considerations

Deploying shards in same Region

The aforementioned deployment using MMS was done on the same region across multiple availability zones. Observe that both the shards in the cluster are running on two different machines, mongod running 27000 has mongo-10 machine as the primary, whereas mongod running on 27001 has mongo-11 machine instance as primary member.

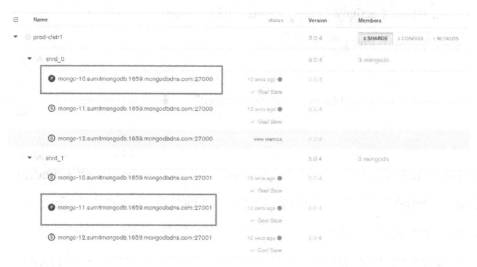

By diversifying the shards in two primary mongod's, at least one shard will have no replication lag thus allowing faster failover to new primary.

Deploying across regions

Multi region deployments are very similar and diversify the availability even farther to what we saw in the multi- zone deployments. The only difference is some members of replica set is running on a separate region.

Multi region deployments give cluster resilience from a single region going down or unavailable. Another advantage is data locality using tag aware sharding. Tag aware sharding allows isolation of operations based on location ,it facilitates data locality to the shards that are geographically closest to the application servers.

Caveat of such a deployment is latency introduced depending on the ping distance between regions.

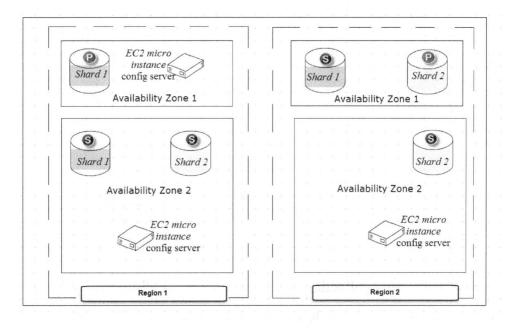

Figure 5.5

There are two ways multi region deployments can be handled. Simplest is to replica of shards in each region for highest data availability even if one region is unavailable due to network partition or any other calamity.

Alternately the whole shard can be deployed on one particular region. In a location-aware deployment, each MongoDB *shard* is localized to a specific region for client application proximity.

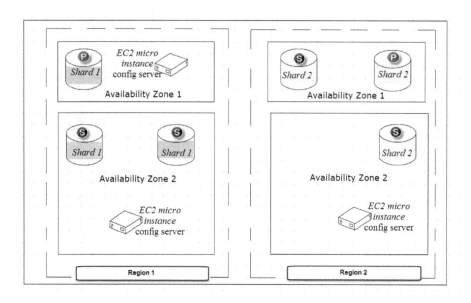

Figure 5.6

Consider the zips collection again, we may want all the data related to west coast to go to a node deployed in west coast . We can use tag based sharding to route all data for state code in CA , OR ,WA etc to go to a shard deployed in us-west region.

Horizontal Scaling – Sharding

MongoDB on AWS

Multi region deployments allow applications to perform local write operations for their data. Also since data is replicated from the other region, local reads becomes a possibility.

Chapter 6

MongoDB Storage on AWS ecosystem

Chapter Objectives

> ➤ *Quick overview of AWS storage options.*
>
> ➤ *MongoDB storage considerations on AWS platform.*
>
> ➤ *MongoDB memory mapped storage engines.*
>
> ➤ *Scaling MongoDB storage on AWS for performance and redundancy.*

....

EC2 Instance storage comes in different flavors depending on the volatility and retention requirements. EC2 default storage is instance store (ephemeral storage), it's a block level storage ideal for temporary storage of information that changes frequently, like buffers, caches etc. Instance storage is located on disks that are physically attached to the host computer (*figure 6.1*). Instance storage

consists of instance stores which are combination of block level devices.

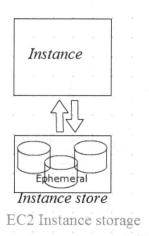

Figure 6.1

Instance store contents persist during the lifetime of a instance, if you stop your instance for any reason or disk drive failure happen the instance store contents are lost. In case of reboots the instance data persists

If you want your data to persist long term it's advisable to use durable AWS data storage solutions like EBS or S3.

EBS

EBS volumes are designed to be primary storage for data that requires frequent updates, such as the system drive for an instance or a database (*figure 6.2*).

MongoDB on AWS

Amazon EBS backed Instance

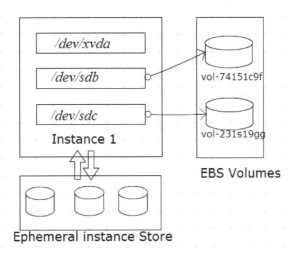

Figure 6.2

Contents of EBS volume persist independent of the life of EC2 instance to which its attached. EBS volume is a block level storage device that can be mapped to a single EC2 instance. Unlike ephemeral Instance storage, EBS is durable and replicated storage. When you create a EBS storage in a availability zone it automatically gets replicated in the same zone to disallow data loss due to hardware failures.

You cannot attach an EBS volume to an instance that's not in the same availability zone or to more than one instance. An EBS backed instance can be stopped and restarted without any issue. The data in the volume persist till the volume is explicitly deleted. From disaster recovery point of view EBS provides backups (or snapshots) of EBS volumes, wherein you can copy the data redundantly in multiple availability zones to amazon simple storage service (commonly referred to as S3). These snapshots are incremental backup in the sense that only the most recently modified data is written to amazon S3.

Simple storage service (S3)

Amazon simple storage service (or S3) is an online storage facility popular for its ease of use and anywhere/anytime availability.S3 is designed for greater than 99% durability and availability.

To store object in amazon S3 a bucket is created. . Buckets are the containers for objects, we can have one or more buckets. For each bucket, we can control access to it (who can create, delete, and list objects in the bucket), view access logs for it and its objects, and choose the geographical region where Amazon S3 will store the bucket and its contents. To store an object in Amazon S3, we upload the file you want to store to a bucket.

S3 is commonly used for Backup and Storage, Application Hosting (deploy, install, and manage web application), or Hosting software applications.

When we create EBS snapshots, they are automatically stored in S3.

Glacier

MongoDB on AWS

Amazon glacier is another online storage solution by Amazon , very similar to S3 in concept but way economical(around 10X cheaper, prices start at $.01 per GB).When data is uploaded on glacier it synchronously stores your data across multiple facilities before confirming a successful upload. Of course with the price cut comes some limitations. It's not for fast retrieval and storage, it's for long term storage in database terms a well suited solution for online data archiving at low price. Apart from being cheaper it automatically encrypts data at rest, Glacier supports data transfer over SSL.

Another limitation (or property if you may call it that) of glacier uploads is data stored is immutable, after an archive is created it cannot be updated.

MongoDB space considerations

Data Files

MongoDB stores the underlying data and metadata in the data directory specified in the config file or specified explicitly during mongod invocation. Each mongod instance will need a data directory associated with it .In the AWS instances we were using either */var/lib/mongo* or */Data* directories. For each database there is a separate file under this directory, each database will have an .ns file associated with it and several data files.

```
# ls -ltr

total 163872

drwx------ 2 mongod mongod    16384 Jun 17 23:38 lost+found

-rw-r--r-- 1 mongod mongod       69 Jun 18 17:45 storage.bson

-rw------- 1 mongod mongod 16777216 Jun 18 17:58 censusdb.ns

-rw------- 1 mongod mongod 67108864 Jun 18 17:58 censusdb.0

drwxr-xr-x 2 mongod mongod     4096 Jun 19 12:39 journal

-rwxr-xr-x 1 mongod mongod        5 Jun 19 12:39 mongod.lock

-rw------- 1 mongod mongod 16777216 Jun 19 12:39 local.ns

-rw------- 1 mongod mongod 67108864 Jun 19 12:39 local.0
```

As your database grows there may be several data files visible in the data directory, these files will have a monotonically increasing numeric suffix. For each new file that's created the size doubles, this is done to ensure small databases do not waste too much disk space.

Journal Files

When enabled with journaling, mongoDB creates special journal files that contain the exact disk location and bytes changed for a write operation. The contents of data files are flushed to disk from virtual memory every 60 seconds, if anything goes wrong while data is still in memory journaling will come to the rescue ,thus it needs to hold approximately 60 seconds worth of write operations.

MongoDB on AWS

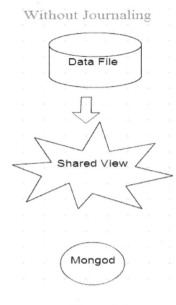

Figure 6.3

When *mongod* is started it maps your data file to a shared view in memory, the view is created in virtual memory. During write operations any changes to this in-memory map will be flushed to corresponding data file during periodic data flushes.

MongoDB on AWS

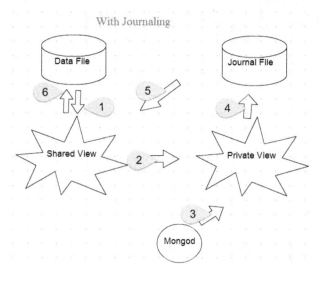

Figure 6.4

With journaling mongod maintains a private mapping. For every write operation *MongoDB* stores and applies write operations to this private map, information about these changes flow to journal file in on-disk journal before the changes are applied to data files residing on disk.

The chronological order of operations in case of journaling enabled is (refer *figure 6.4* for context)

1. *Mongod* is started and data file is mapped to shared view.

2. When journaling is enabled, a private view is created and shared view is mapped to private view. Private view is not connected to data files.

3. As write operation arrives , its written to private view.

4. The write operation is written to journal file, describing which byte in what file has changed due to incoming write. At this point the write is in safekeeping of journal .Even if *mongod* goes down for any reason, the write can be replayed to data files since it's already logged in journal file.

5. Journal applies the changes to Shared view.

6. Shared view once again remaps its contents to private view to keep them at sync and applies these changes to data file during next flush.

To enable journals *Mongod* needs to be started with *--journal* command line option. Journals make sure that the consistency of the on-disk journal files is preserved. When journaling is enabled, *MongoDB* creates a journal subdirectory within the directory defined by dbPath, which is */data/db* by default (or whatever is overridden by entry in */etc/mongo.confd* file). The journal directory contains write-ahead redo logs (or Journal files).

Journal files are append-only files and have file names prefixed with *j._*. *MongoDB* creates a new journal file every 1 GB of data. If you have ever observed your data directory it holds a last-sequence-number file as well. One way to find out if your last shutdown was clean or not is to look at Journal directory. A clean shutdown cleans files from the journal directory, if we find remnants of files in the journal directory the shutdown was anything but clean.

Note: Never remove these files as they are used to automatically recover the database to a consistent state when the mongod is restarted.

Usually journal directory should contain only two or three journal files.

Journal files are needed for recovery purposes and are temporary in nature. As soon as all the write operations in a particular journal file are applied to the database data files, MongoDB deletes the file.

If you see your Journal becoming too big,

- o execute the *db.fsynclock()* command to flush the changes in journal files to disk .Once the changes make it to disk the corresponding journal files are not needed and they would be deleted.

- o Unlock the database again using *db.fsyncUnlock()* and mongod is again ready to receive write operations

We already track/log the operations in oplog how is that different from journals?

Oplogs are machine readable logs that help in data redundancy when used with replica set. Journaling on the other hand is more human readable and need to be applied to each instance separately.

File system snapshots

File system snapshots are "block-level" backup strategy to create copies *MongoDB's* data files. File system snapshots uses system level tools, these methods require more system configuration outside of *MongoDB*. File systems snapshots are not a specific to mongoDB but are an operating system volume manager feature. The snapshot methodology will depend on the underlying storage system.

Ex: in on-premise (and EC2) Linux systems the LVM manager can create a snapshot. In AWS you can also create snapshots from EBS backed volumes we will look at this use case in sections that follow.

For snapshot to be successful all writes accepted by the database need to be fully written either to the journal or to data files. Any writes not on disk already when backup begins, the backup will not reflect these changes. Snapshots create an image of an entire disk image. It's a recommended practice to logically partition your Data files and journals in disk to isolate your backups based on these logical units.

MongoDB storage on AWS

Unless you don't want your data to persist when you shut down your EC2 instance (for whatever reasons), Ephemeral storage is not a good choice since it volatile in persistence and contents are lost when instances are terminated. For your production deployments at a minimum use EBS backed instances. For best results use Provisioned IOPS EBS volumes.

Generally EBS volumes are good candidates for data, journal and Log directories. It's recommended to take periodic snapshots of EBS volumes , snapshots go to S3 buckets by default. If any other archiving solution is used it can be stored in S3 for fast retrieval or to Glacier for long-term stowage (similar to tape storage in traditional on-premise databases)

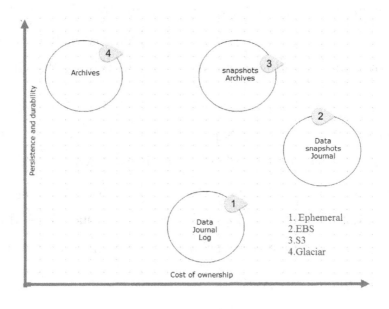

Figure 6.5

MongoDB Storage on AWS ecosystem

MongoDB on AWS

General purpose EBS volumes offer 4-5 millisecond latencies and can scale upto 160 MB/s of I/O throughput. With provisioned IOPS EBS volumes the throughput ceiling is almost double to 320 MB/s. There is always an option of scaling the IOPS by using multiple EBS volumes.

The table below shows a comparison of SSD volume types

	General Purpose	Provisioned IOPS
Usage	Used for System boot volumes and for deploying Development and test environments	Ideal for production MongoDB applications that require sustained IOPS performance, or more than 10,000 IOPS or 160 MiB/s of throughput per volume
Maximum throughput	160 MiB/s	320 MiB/s
IOPS performance	Starting from 3 IOPS/GiB scaling up to 10,000 IOPS.	Can scale up to 20,000 IOPS maximum

Since the *MongoDB* data elements have different refresh frequency and change ratings, it's recommended to use separate volumes for data , journal, and the log files. Keeping them separate allows for better management of I/O contention.

Memory mapped storage engine

Storage engine is responsible for managing data storage on disk. For MongoDB *MMAPv1* is the default storage engine. The storage engine in MongoDB 3.0 is an improved version of its predecessor with support for collection level concurrency control.

There is choice of upgrading to *WiredTiger* storage engine in 3.0. *WiredTiger* storage engine supports document level concurrency control. *WiredTiger* results in lower storage costs and optimal hardware utilization.

Due to difference in granularity of concurrency control, how *MongoDB* writes data to disk differ based on what storage engine is used.

Since *MMAPv1* uses collection level concurrency control for sake of atomicity ,MongoDB records all operations in a journal. The journal is written to disk more frequently than data to data files. When using *MMAPv1*, the journal should always be enabled. This allows the database to recover in case of an involuntary shutdown.

WiredTiger on the other hand rewrites the whole document. For data persistence *WiredTiger* uses both checkpoints and write ahead logs.

Another difference between *MMAPv1* and *WiredTiger* is how object reside in memory for these two engines. *MMAPv1* stores memory mapped files and WiredTiger manages objects using in memory cache. When using EBS backed volumes that limit block sizes, we need to make sure our read ahead settings are optimal. Having a large read ahead setting will cause more data to be loaded to memory, jolting other data from memory that may be required for applications.

When read or write happens on an object, object needs to be in memory. If not residing in memory page fault (in case of *MMAPv1*) and cache miss (in case of *WiredTiger*) takes place to make room in the memory for the desired data object.

Scaling MongoDB storage on AWS

EBS with RAID10 configuration

RAID10 provides protection for the storage along with faster performance. RAID10 provides the data protection by stripping and mirroring the data across two disks. In RAID1 configuration information is preserved even if one disk drive fails , as mirrored data resides on the redundant disk. RAID0 provides faster write performance as bits are written in succession to the disks.

Combination of both 1 and 0 is RAID10 configuration thus information is available in more than 1 disk and read/write performance is faster.

For high durability its recommended to use RAID 10 on EBS volumes with following configuration (*figure 6.6*).

- Four volumes for the */data* directory.

- RAID 1 mirror for */journal* directory.

- RAID1 mirror for */log* directory.

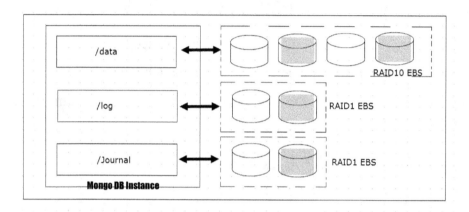

Figure 6.6

EBS with RAID0 configuration

In large production clusters where replica set may have multiple secondary nodes, replica set itself takes care of data durability. The performance of storage subsystem may suffer in these large clusters

.It's worth considering sacrificing durability for performance. Instead of using RAID10 we can use RAID 0 stripe set for */data* directory. [5]

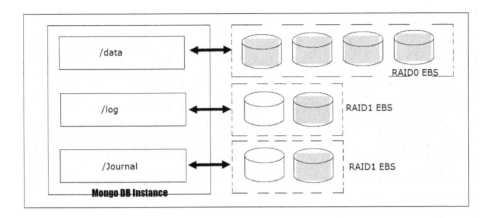

Figure 6.7

---

[5] Refer this page for more information on how to build RAID arrays on EC2 Linux instances
http://docs.aws.amazon.com/AWSEC2/latest/UserGuide/raid-config.html

MongoDB Storage on AWS ecosystem

Chapter 7

Backup and Restore

Chapter Objectives

➢ *Understanding MongoDB command line utilities*
  mongodump and mongorestore.

➢ *Backup and recovery using EBS snapshots, using EC2*
  Console and AWS CLI.

➢ *Using MMS to schedule backups.*

➢ *Restore database using MMS.*

....

Backup and recovery strategy is needed for mission critical *MongoDB* deployments to safeguard against data loss due to natural disasters and accidental data deletion. Combination of AWS geographic spread and replica set reduces the risk of data unavailability but it does not prevent from data loss or is not a disaster recovery solution. For some business application owners it is essential practice from regulatory requirements to regularly backup and archives the data in for longer term retention . For other businesses they need at least X months' worth of data for analytics and cannot afford disruption due to data loss.

The backup and recovery strategy should be driven by two parameters, specific to your business goals.

o Understand the appetite of your business for volume of data loss, in other words how much data your organization is willing to lose. Also known as recovery point objective (RPO)

o How much times will it to take to recover the data in case of loss. Also known as recovery time objective (RTO)

Data should be evaluated on application to application level to understand where the data stands in these two important parameters (RPO and RTO).

mongodump and mongorestore

mongodump is a backup utility shipped with all *MongoDB* distributions. *mongodump* utility works through the query mechanism and dumps all the documents a *MongoDB* server contains to a disk. *mongodump* can produce a consistent snapshot of the data by dumping the *oplog*. You can then use the *mongorestore* utility to restore the data to a new or existing database.

mongodump may be an ideal approach for small deployments, it may not be suitable for larger systems. The snapshot *mongodump* creates are not point in time and running *mongodump* results in slight performance degradation on the *MongoDB* server while it's running. Since *mongodump* does not work on an incremental approach, it requires a complete dump at each snapshot point , this makes it resource-hogging operation.

mongorestore imports content from the BSON database dumps produced by mongodump and replay the oplog. mongodump creates. BSON works with both of *WiredTiger* and *MMAPv1* storage engines.

For mongodump you can attach another EBS backed volume on your instance and mount it on a seperate */backup* directory.

Backup using mongodump: To backup contents of *censusdb* database that contains zips collection

```
# mongodump -d censusdb -o /backup

2015-06-18T17:59:15.528+0000    writing censusdb.zips to /backup/censusdb/zips.bson

2015-06-18T17:59:15.528+0000    writing censusdb.system.indexes to
/backup/censusdb/system.indexes.bson

2015-06-18T17:59:15.643+0000    writing censusdb.zips metadata to
/backup/censusdb/zips.metadata.json

2015-06-18T17:59:15.644+0000    done dumping censusdb.zips
```

Check the contents of */backup* directory where the database was dumped, observe the *zips.bson* file, this file contains the contents of zips collection in BSON format that mongoDB uses to store data internally.

```
# cd /backup

[root@ip-172-31-63-100 backup]# ls

censusdb  test

[root@ip-172-31-63-100 backup]# cd censusdb/

[root@ip-172-31-63-100 censusdb]# ls

system.indexes.bson  zips.bson  zips.metadata.json
```

Recovery using mongorestore: To restore the database to a new database (*censusdb_new*) , provide the following command with the path of the backup directory

mongorestore -d censusdb_new /backup/censusdb

```
# mongorestore -d censusdb_new /backup/censusdb

2015-06-18T18:39:45.896+0000    building a list of collections to restore from
/backup/censusdb dir

2015-06-18T18:39:45.897+0000    reading metadata file from
/backup/censusdb/zips.metadata.json

2015-06-18T18:39:45.897+0000    restoring censusdb_new.zips from file
/backup/censusdb/zips.bson

2015-06-18T18:39:46.446+0000    restoring indexes for collection censusdb_new.zips
from metadata

2015-06-18T18:39:46.446+0000    finished restoring censusdb_new.zips

2015-06-18T18:39:46.446+0000    done
```

Backup and Restore

To take backup of zip collection alone, we can specify collection name after *--c* option.

Backup of individual collection: For this backup exercise we will route contents of zip collection to a different subdirectory (*/backup/collectionBackup*) maintained specific for collection level backups.

```
# mongodump -d censusdb -c zips -o /backup/collectionBackup

2015-06-18T18:23:16.606+0000   writing censusdb.zips to
/backup/collectionBackup/censusdb/zips.bson

2015-06-18T18:23:16.796+0000   writing censusdb.zips metadata to
/backup/collectionBackup/censusdb/zips.metadata.json

2015-06-18T18:23:16.797+0000   done dumping censusdb.zips
```

Having control of backup at the collection level allows the backup schedule to vary based on how often the collection data changes.

EBS Snapshot using EC2 Console

We can back up *MongoDB* by copying the underlying files that the database uses to store data. When you create data directory on EC2 instance, create a EBS backed volume and mount it on */data* directory .EBS snapshots are taken at the storage level, file system snapshots can be a more efficient approach than *mongodump* for taking full backups and restoring them. However, unlike mongodump we lose the flexibility to backup specific databases.

A file system backup like *EBS snapshot* can only be restored to a *MongoDB* deployment running the same storage engine as the deployment from which the snapshot was taken.

EBS snapshot does give the advantage of doing the recovery much easily using point and click GUI functionality. Consider a scenario where you want to restore a database to a different instance than the current instance in the same availability zone. With an EBS snapshot the process can be completed in few clicks. You can also use AWS command line tool to accomplish backup/restore. Whatever method we choose we will need to lock the database to allow point in time snapshots for the data residing in */data*.

1. ***Locking the database:*** Lock the database using *fsync* command. *fsync* command makes sure all pending writes in memory are flushed to */data* directory. This is a kind of exclusive lock that prevents further writes to the database till it's unlocked again.

   fsync allows the flexibility of taking backups without shutting down the server. Once locked by *fsync* the data directory contents are consistent, point in time snapshots of database data.

```
> use admin

switched to db admin

> db.runCommand({fsync:1,lock:1});

{

    "info" : "now locked against writes, use db.fsyncUnlock() to unlock",

    "seeAlso" : "http://dochub.mongodb.org/core/fsynccommand",

    "ok" : 1

}
```

2. Check the data directory from dbPath in the configuration file
   /etc/mongod.conf.

3. Check the volume using mount.

```
$ mount

/dev/xvdb on /data type ext4 (rw,noexec,noatime,data=ordered)
```

*Note : When EBS volumes are attached, the devices that show as
sd* are actually symlinks of xv*. The data directory is mounted
on /dev/xvdb . which corresponds to block device /dev/sdb (
check the instance details in AWS EC2 console, it should show
up in the description tab)*

4. Click on the block device to see the volume id.

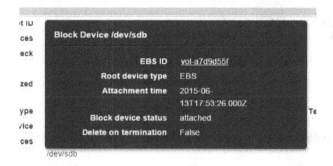

5. From the navigator on the left hand select the volume.

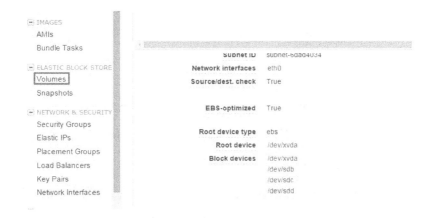

6. Click on the volume Id and from actions menu choose create snapshot.

7. Snapshot will be visible in the snapshots menu (below *volumes* under *"Elastic Block Store"*).

8. Once snapshot is created database can be unlocked for write operations.

```
> db.$cmd.sys.unlock.findOne();

{ "ok" : 1, "info" : "unlock completed" }
```

9. The snapshot that we created is not going to cost us the same as EBS volume. The snapshots are stored on S3, and thus charges are based S3 storage costs. The snapshot data backup is compressed, thus if we took a backup of EBS volume 1 TB in size the snapshot will less than 1 TB.

EBS Snapshot using AWS CLI

There is no way to schedule snapshots using EC2 console,EC2 console is convenient when doing adhoc manual snapshot and restore. To schedule the EBS snapshots using custom scripts AWS CLI is used. [6] The *"aws ec2 create-snapshot"* command creates a snapshot of an EBS backed volume using AWS CLI.

aws ec2 create-snapshot --volume-id vol-88e9ec41 --description "MongoDB data volume snapshot."

---

[6] refer chapter 2 for quick reference on how to configure AWS CLI on EC2 instances . For detailed information Refer
https://docs.aws.amazon.com/AWSEC2/latest/CommandLineReference/set-up-ec2-cli-linux.html.

Backup and Restore

MongoDB on AWS

It takes the volume Id of the EC2 volume (in this case ***vol-88e9ec41***) used for */data* directory.

The output of the EC2 create snapshot list the following contents.

SnapshotId: System generated ID of the snapshot.

VolumeId: The ID of the volume used for snapshot.

VolumeSize: The size of the volume in GiB.

State: snapshot state.

OwnerId : AWS account ID of the EBS snapshot owner.

Description: The user defined description for the snapshot.

```
# aws ec2 create-snapshot --volume-id vol-88e9ec41 --description "MongoDB
data volume snapshot."
{
    "Description": "MongoDB data volume snapshot.",
    "Tags": [],
    "VolumeId": " vol-88e9ec41",
    "State": "pending",
    "VolumeSize": 100,
    "StartTime": "2015-07-25T21:08:14.000Z",
    "OwnerId": "678884037580",
    "SnapshotId": " snap-81b9eff6 "
}
```

```
    }
```

There are multiple ways to create wrapper scripts around the AWS CLI to automate this process .Please refer one such sample script from *github*.

https://github.com/colinbjohnson/aws-missing-tools/tree/master/ec2-automate-backup

Restoring Volume using EC2 Console

As part database recovery from an existing backup , EC2 console can be used to build a new volume from an existing EBS snapshot .

1. Create a new volume using the snapshot , select the snapshot and select actions→create volume

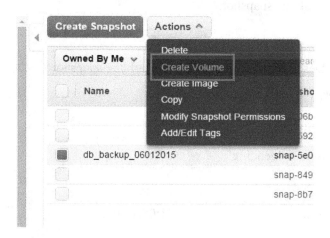

2. There will be new volume visible in the volume menu with state as creating

The state will change to available once its created

3. We can attach the newly created volume to any instance , and mount volume to data directory to be used as the new database data repository

To attach the new volume for data directory follow the same process we executed during manual launching of standalone *MongoDB* instance.

Restoring Volume using AWS CLI

To restore a Volume using an existing EBS snapshot using command line utilities we will use AWS CLI again.

The *"aws ec2 create-volume"* command creates a provisioned IOPS SSD volume using an existing snapshot.

aws ec2 create-volume --region us-east-1 --availability-zone us-east-1e --snapshot-id snap-81b9eff6 --volume-type io1 --iops 500

This command can be useful even when deploying a *MongoDB* EC2 instance on a separate region using /data volume of an existing EC2 instance.

The output of the EC2 create volume list the following contents.

- *VolumeId*: The ID of the volume (Created by restoration process).

- *Size*: The size of the volume being created (in GiBs.)

o *SnapshotId*: source snapshot creating the volume.

o *VolumeType*: io1 for Provisioned IOPS (SSD) volumes, or standard for Magnetic volumes.

o *Iops*: For Provisioned IOPS (SSD) volume gives the number of IOPS that are provisioned for the volume.

```
# aws ec2 create-volume --region us-east-1 --availability-zone us-east-1e --
snapshot-id snap-81b9eff6 --volume-type io1 --iops 500
{
    "AvailabilityZone": "us-east-1e",
    "Attachments": [],
    "Tags": [],
    "VolumeType": "io1",
    "VolumeId": " vol-7efcd890",
    "State": "creating",
    "Iops": 1000,
    "SnapshotId": " snap-81b9eff6 ",
    "CreateTime": "2015-07-25T21:15:14.000Z",
    "Size": 500
}
```

Backups from slave

Snapshot backups can be executed on any instance that has EBS backed volumes. Even the secondary members contain copy of the same data being written to master. Using slave or secondary members as backup sources gives greater flexibility as locking slaves most often do not result in any system bottlenecks.

Most often the client applications using secondary members for read requests tend to have longer SLA windows. If near real-time reads are required always use the default preference of using primary member for read requests.

When using slave for backups , we are free to shut down the instance or lock the database for write requests while taking backups, the performance degradation during backups is of minor importance.

Using MMS for Backup/restore

MongoDB management service (or MMS in short) is a service for managing *MongoDB* infrastructure. One feature it provides is scheduling of point in time of *MongoDB* databases.

MMS installs a lightweight agent on the MongoDB infrastructure and backups up data from replica set or standalone members.

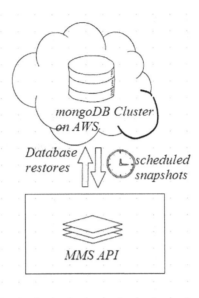

Figure 7.1

During backup using MMS, the agent performs an initial sync of a data in a similar fashion as a hidden member would do when added to a replica set. The agent sends this data and *oplog* contents over the internet to MMS. Agent uses standard *MongoDB* queries to "shadow" the oplog of replica set and keep the backup copy in sync. This shadowing is invisible to the replica set.

MMS takes the snapshot of data every 6 hours by default, the setting can be changed. the snapshots that MMS creates need to be scheduled , it doesn't allow on demand backups. Retention policy of backed up data is also tied to frequency of your snapshot.

Backup and Restore

MMS also provides option to exclude databases and backups that you may not want to back up like logs or temporary collections, allowing to reduce the backup size and cost associated with that.

For backups MMS uses *MMAPv1* by default .If taking snapshots in MongoDB 3.0 or higher we can choose between *MMAPv1* and *WiredTiger* for storage engine. There is no restriction that the storage engine for a backup match that of the data it replicates,If our deployment is with *MMAPv1* we can choose to take backup using *WiredTiger* and vice versa.

For restoring the backup in sharded cluster we can use MMS to restore from checkpoints between snapshots. For replica sets, we can use points in time snapshots for restore.

Remember MMS is separate from AWS and has its own redundancy mechanism. Failures that affect AWS will not affect the MMS infrastructure, both are not linked.

1. Select the backup tab and select start

2. For backup to start you need to have agent running on the node that needs to be backed up.

3. On the enable backup page, select the cluster you need to backup. We launched the sharded cluster in the previous chapters using MMS. We will use that for backup.

4. For the sync source we can choose a primary or any secondary node. The requirements for secondary node are that it should not be hidden or delayed. Its recommended to use secondary for backup to reduce impact on read/write traffic volume on primary due to backup.

5. In the advanced setting we can specify the storage engine to be used for backup

6. We can also exclude any database or collection, we deem unfit for backup.

When backup is enabled you would see agent doing an intial sync of the data from the config and replication setups.

If we have any issues during previous backups or we need to do a unscheduled backup we can always do a manual resync.

To restore a cluster , click on the cluster name→options→restore

On the next screen ,Click on the snapshot to be used for restore

On the next screen , choose whether you want to push or pull the

restore. When you use Pull Via Secure HTTP MMS creates one-time direct download link. The option lets you know the size of the compressed file and size of decompressed backup file.

If push via secure copy is chosen, Cloud Manager copies the restore files to mongoDB server via SCP.

The option allows using the following formats for restore

o *Individual DB Files*: Cloud manager uploads MongoDB data directly to the target directory. Cloud manager uses compressed data during data transfer

o *Archive (tar.gz)*: If your database is huge , this option allows transmission of database files in a single tar.gz file. The files need to be uncompressed before database restore.

Chapter 8

Monitoring

Chapter Objectives

> ➢ *Monitor the MongoDB statistics using command line utilities at cluster, database and operations level.*

> ➢ *Monitoring cluster statistics using MMS GUI.*

> ➢ *Usage of AWS CloudWatch to monitor EC2 instances and publishing custom metrics to CloudWatch.*

> ➢ *Using CloudWatch alarms to trigger events based on system threshold.*

....

Cluster monitoring can vary in granularity , ranging from EC2 instance metrics to command line utilities from *MongoDB* for database specific metrics. We can also use AWS and MMS to schedule EC2 and database specific alerts.

Cluster statistics

mongostat: To view activities inside your cluster use *mongostat* utility that's shipped with mongoDB installs. *mongostat* provides a window on what's happening in the cluster. When having doubts about your clusters performance or issues with MongoDB cluster,start by looking at *mongostat*.

```
[ec2-user@mongo-10 bin]$ /var/lib/mongodb-mms-automation/mongodb-linux-
x86_64-3.0.4/bin/mongostat

insert query update delete getmore command flushes mapped  vsize  res faults
qr|qw ar|aw netIn netOut conn set repl     time

 212  1   23   *0    0   15|0    0      256.0M 8.0M   0  0|0  0|0 885b
10k  10     RTR 23:20:02

  71  1   11   *0    0    4|0    0      256.0M 8.0M   0  0|0  0|0 245b
6k  11     RTR 23:20:03
```

Mongostat output provides the following details

- o *flushes* – By default MongoDB writes data from memory to disk
  every 60 seconds. Flushes show how often mongod is flushing
  data to disk.

- o *faults* – MongoDB maintains a subset of data in memory ,
  known as memory set. When a new operation arrives fata is
  checked in working set for faster retrieval. If data is not found in
  working set , data is loaded from disk and oldest used data is
  bounced from memory to make space. The faults column shows
  you the number of Linux page faults per second. High values
  mean we need bigger RAM to accommodate a larger working
  set.

Monitoring

o *locked %* – This metric states the percent of global write lock. A larger value of locked% means the database is not available for any other operation. Needless to say a higher value more often will result in slow performance of cluster.

o *qr|qw* – qr and qw stand for read and write queues respectively. Like any other operational system any read write traffic is queued if it can't be assigned the necessary resources. qr|qw stands for number of read and writes waiting in queue due to some long running queries/operations that's keeping resources busy. When this value increases its time to stop submitting any more operations to mongoDB to stabilize the queue. Queues generally elongate during write heavy operations.

mongotop: Equivalent to top utility for Linux systems. Using *mongotop* admins can evaluate the amount of time a *MongoDB* instance is busy reading and writing. *mongotop* returns values every second and for each collection

ns	total	read	write	2015-07-01T13:12:11-14:00
admin.system.roles	0ms	0ms	0ms	
admin.system.version	0ms	0ms	0ms	
local.me	0ms	0ms	0ms	
local.oplog.rs	0ms	0ms	0ms	

Monitoring

- .
- .
- .

Database statistics

db.stats() provides the statistics for a specific database.

```
db.stats()
{
    "db" : "censusdb",
    "collections" : 3,
    "objects" : 20004,
    "avgObjSize" : 111.99040191961608,
    "dataSize" : 2240256,
    "storageSize" : 2805760,
    "numExtents" : 7,
    "indexes" : 1,
    "indexSize" : 531440,
    "fileSize" : 67108864,
    "nsSizeMB" : 16,
    "extentFreeList" : {
        "num" : 9,
```

```
        "totalSize" : 13934592
    },
    "dataFileVersion" : {
        "major" : 4,
        "minor" : 22
    },
    "ok" : 1,
    "$gleStats" : {
        "lastOpTime" : Timestamp(0, 0),
        "electionId" : ObjectId("55967aac8882c9836a937d77")
    }
}
```

- *db* :Name of the database

- *collections*: Number signifying total number of collections in the database.

- *objects*: Number signifying total documents across all collections in the database.

- *avgObjectSize*: averae size of the objects , calculated as sum(size of all object sin a collection)/count(documents in database).

- o *dataSize* :Total size of the data held across all the collections in the database

- o *indexes*: count of indexes across all collections in the database.

- o *indexSize*: Size in bytes of all indexes in the database.

Collection statistics

To drill down on the collection stats regarding space and memory usage use collection stats. Ex: To check stats for *statecensus* collection simply we can use *db.statecensus.stats()*

```
          db.statecensus.stats()
{

    "ns" : "test.statecensus",

    "count" : 0,

    "size" : 0,

    "numExtents" : 1,

    "storageSize" : 8192,

    "lastExtentSize" : 8192,

    "paddingFactor" : 1,

    "paddingFactorNote" : "paddingFactor is unused and unmaintained in 3.0.
It remains hard coded to 1.0 for compatibility only.",

    "userFlags" : 1,
```

Monitoring

```
        "capped" : false,

        "nindexes" : 2,

        "totalIndexSize" : 16352,

        "indexSizes" : {

            "_id_" : 8176,

            "state_1_zip_1" : 8176

        },

        "ok" : 1,

        "$gleStats" : {

            "lastOpTime" : Timestamp(0, 0),

            "electionId" : ObjectId("55967aac8882c9836a937d77")

        }

    }
```

Operation statistics

To check the current operations in progress, we can use *db.currentOp()* . This method provides list of all operations in progress . In case you are interested to what's bogging down the *MongoDB* servers this command comes handy.

```
mongos> db.currentOp()

{
```

```json
"inprog" : [

    {

        "desc" : "conn21",

        "threadId" : "0x2b47dc0",

        "connectionId" : 21,

        "opid" : "shrd_0:181416",

        "active" : true,

        "secs_running" : 4,

        "microsecs_running" : NumberLong(4425278),

        "op" : "getmore",

        "ns" : "local.oplog.rs",

        "query" : {

            "ts" : {

                "$gte" : Timestamp(1435528801, 1)

            }

        },

        "client_s" : "172.31.32.133:36643",

        "numYields" : 0,

        "locks" : {

        },

        "waitingForLock" : false,
```

```
"lockStats" : {

    "Global" : {

        "acquireCount" : {

            "r" : NumberLong(10)

        }

    }

.............
```

- o *opid* – operation id also reveals the shard the operation is running on. To kill an operation simply pass the *opid* to *db.killop* method.

```
mongos> db.killOp("shrd_1:187669")
{ "op" : "shrd_1:187669", "shard" : "shrd_1", "shardid" : 187669 }
```

- o *active* – reveals the state of the operation.

- o *op* – the operation type (insert, remove etc).

- o *ns* –Namespace operation is operating upon ,in *database.collection* format.

- o *query* –query being executed

o *secs_running* –operation run-time in seconds .

Monitoring using MMS

MMS agents running on the cluster send the stats on a secure channel to MMS monitoring interface. MMS provides the functionality to watch the cluster performance at a time granularity of 1 min.

MMS monitoring capabilities range from very basic (manual monitoring) to more nuanced (automated alerts).

At the basic level we can look at performance metric of the sharded cluster as a whole by looking at Performance metric dashboard (*"actions* ➔*Performance metric"*)

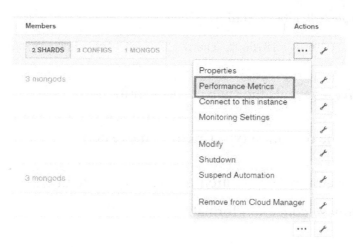

Monitoring

We can glance at *MongoDB* statistics from different levels using the charts drop down menu.

Time granularity of the charts can also be set , ranging from 1 hour to 1 day.we can also get the breakup of the charts for individual nodes to average out for the shard as a whole. For a replica set monitoring can be focused to look at metrics at the individual node level.

Ex : *mongo-10* instance is the primary instance of our replica set , if we want to look at Opcounters or PageFaults we can select the *"Actions →Performance metric"* for an individual EC2 instance.

Above screen grab is displaying the *Opcounters* for mongo10 instance.

We can slice and dice the monitoring metric at hardware and database level by choosing the appropriate view.

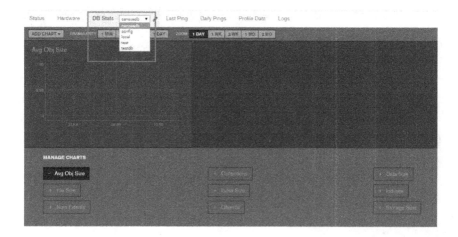

The above screen grab is looking at individual database statistics on the *"DB Stats"* view.

At an advanced level alerts can also be set using MMS , alerts trigger an Email or SMS to send notification to the delivery list or production support in case of any predefined events.

To set parameters for alert mechanism ,go to *Activity* tab, there will be host of activities visible in the activity window.

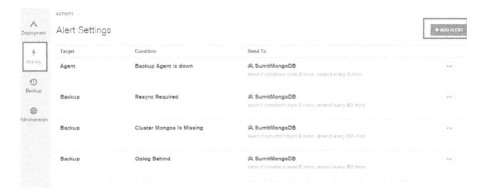

Click on Add alert on the upper right corner

A new pop up will open, the window allows us to customize the alerts based on our needs.

Add the alert condition

We will add an alert for the replica set, the condition would be if any member of our 3 member replica set goes down, we want automatic notification of the event.

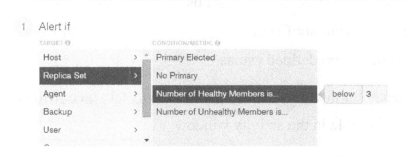

Add the replica set to be monitored

If we have more than one replica set we can customize which system we want to choose.

Add the alert delivery mode

We can customize how we want to send the alert

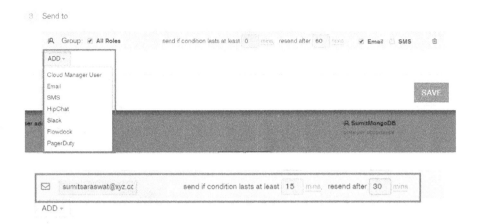

We also added the time threshold for which the condition should last before we start sending emails (15 Minutes) and frequency of emails (will be sent every 30 minutes when exception condition are satisfied). saved alerts will be visible in the home screen for *activity* tab.[7]

---

[7] Refer the following blog post on mongodb.com for ideas on MMS alerts
https://www.mongodb.com/blog/post/five-mms-monitoring-alerts-keep-your-mongodb-deployment-track

MongoDB on AWS

ACTIVITY

Alert Settings

Target	Condition	Send To
Replica Set	Replica Set Number of Healthy Members is below 3	SumitMongoDB
		send if condition lasts 15 mins, resend every 30 mins
		sumitsaraswat@xyz.com
		send if condition lasts 15 mins, resend every 30 mins

Monitoring using AWS Cloud watch

Amazon CloudWatch is basically a metrics repository maintained for each EC2 instance. An AWS product—such as Amazon EC2—puts metrics into the repository, and you retrieve statistics based on those metrics. If you put your own custom metrics into the repository, you can retrieve those statistics as well.

1. Login to cloud watch console for AWS

2. In the metrics tab on he left select the EC2 instances

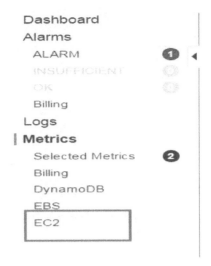

3. Select the metric we want to monitor using cloud watch , here we want to monitor the CPU utilization and Disk write OPS for the EC2 instance mongo-10 that serves the primary member for the sharded cluster

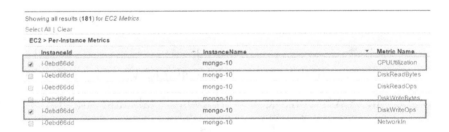

Following screen grabs shows the CPU utilization for the EC2 instance.

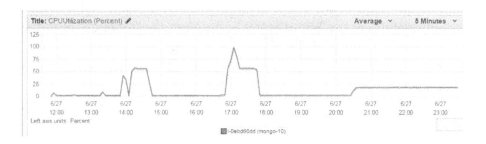

The below screen grab shows the disk write operations on the EC2 instance (straight line) w.r.t CPU Utilization. The graph shows write operations to disk remained 0, in other words there was no paging to disk.

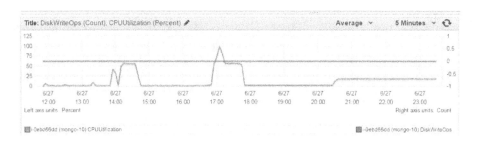

We can watch all the metrics in a single view by selecting on any instance in AWS console, *"monitoring"* tab and viewing the related cloud watch metrics for the instance.[8]

---

[8] For more information on nuances of CloudWatch please refer the AWS documentation. https://docs.aws.amazon.com/AmazonCloudWatch/latest/DeveloperGuide/QuickStartEC2Instance.html

CloudWatch custom metrics (using monitoring scripts)

We can view custom matrices and submit them to *CloudWatch*. These matrices are submitted to CloudWatch via API request.

1. Install the monitoring scripts the first time

```
# sudo yum install perl-DateTime perl-Sys-Syslog perl-LWP-Protocol-https
```

2. *"Dependency Installed"* message, indicates the scripts are installed.

```
Dependency Installed:

:

:

perl-Try-Tiny.noarch 0:0.12-2.5.amzn1              perl-URI.noarch 0:1.60-
9.8.amzn1                 perl-WWW-RobotRules.noarch 0:6.02-5.12.amzn1

   perl-libwww-perl.noarch 0:6.05-2.17.amzn1
```

> Complete!

3. Create a directory to store the scripts and download the zipped collection of scripts.

```
cd cloudwatchScripts/

[root@ip-172-31-51-225 cloudwatchScripts]# wget http://aws-cloudwatch.s3.amazonaws.com/downloads/CloudWatchMonitoringScripts-1.2.1.zip

:

:

:

[root@ip-172-31-51-225 cloudwatchScripts]# ls

CloudWatchMonitoringScripts-1.2.1.zip
```

4. Unzip the zipped folder

```
unzip CloudWatchMonitoringScripts-1.2.1.zip

Archive: CloudWatchMonitoringScripts-1.2.1.zip

extracting: aws-scripts-mon/awscreds.template

inflating: aws-scripts-mon/AwsSignatureV4.pm

inflating: aws-scripts-mon/CloudWatchClient.pm

inflating: aws-scripts-mon/LICENSE.txt
```

```
inflating: aws-scripts-mon/mon-get-instance-stats.pl

inflating: aws-scripts-mon/mon-put-instance-data.pl

inflating: aws-scripts-mon/NOTICE.txt
```

5. Go to subfolder *aws-scripts-mon,* following files will be visible.

```
ls -ltr

total 96

-rw-r--r-- 1 root root   138 Mar  6 22:57 NOTICE.txt

-rwxr-xr-x 1 root root 18144 Mar  6 22:57 mon-put-instance-data.pl

-rwxr-xr-x 1 root root  9739 Mar  6 22:57 mon-get-instance-stats.pl

-rw-r--r-- 1 root root  9124 Mar  6 22:57 LICENSE.txt

-r--r--r-- 1 root root 22487 Mar  6 22:57 CloudWatchClient.pm

-r--r--r-- 1 root root 17021 Mar  6 22:57 AwsSignatureV4.pm

-rw-r--r-- 1 root root    30 Mar  6 22:57 awscreds.template
```

6. We will need to provide secret access key details to submit the metrics to CloudWatch associated with the account. Rename the template file *awscreds.template* to *awscreds.conf* .

```
# cp awscreds.template awscreds.conf
```

Provide the *access key id* and *secret access key* associated with the account[9]

Now we are ready to submit the custom metric to *CloudWatch* .If we want to view the memory utilization and memory available for our MongoDB EC2 instance every 2 hours, these metrics will help us understand how heavily applications are using the database. We can schedule the script with arguments *--mem-util(for memory utilized) and --mem-avail (for memory available)*

```
#./mon-put-instance-data.pl --mem-util --mem-avail


Successfully reported metrics to CloudWatch. Reference Id: 54cc8d76-31a3-
11e5-9df0-877867f2dba9
```

Navigate to *https://console.aws.amazon.com/cloudwatch/.*

We should be able to observe the custom metrices.Under Linux System tab , the custom metrices we just posted are available.

---

[9] If you don't remember these, go to *https://console.aws.amazon.com/iam/home#users* and users menu. Click on the user and under user actions→manage access keys click on create access key.

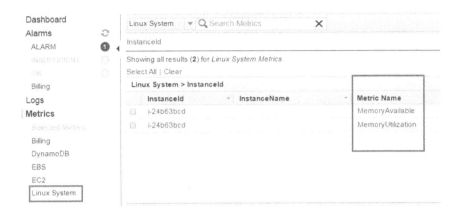

Select any metric to view the graph associated with them.

Monitoring alarms.

What happens if our MongoDB node is breaching memory threshold, it may be time to add more shards, but we need an automated system to let us know when that memory threshold is crossed.

We can set Alarms on MongoDB EC2 Instance and set the criteria when the alarm is applicable. While still in *https://console.aws.amazon.com/cloudwatch/*

1. Click on *"Create Alarm"*

Monitoring

MongoDB on AWS

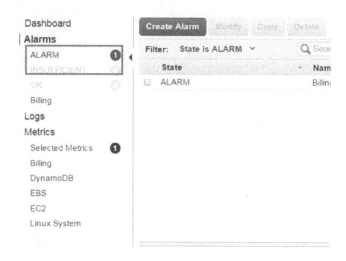

2. Select the metric on which the alarm is desired , in this exercise it is "*memory utilized*"

3. The next step is to define the alarm

1. Select Metric **2. Define Alarm**

Alarm Threshold

Provide the details and threshold for your alarm. Use the graph on the right to help set the appropriate threshold.

Name: MemoryThreshold

Description:

Whenever: MemoryUtilization

is: > ▼ 80

for: 1 consecutive period(s)

Alarm Preview

This alarm will trigger when the blue line goes above the red line for a duration of 5 minutes

MemoryUtilization > 80

Actions

Define what actions are taken when your alarm changes state.

Notification   Delete

Namespace: System/Linux

InstanceId: i-24b63bcd

Metric Name: MemoryUtilization

We set the alarm to send a notification to the email list [10]whenever the memory utilization is more than 80% for a duration of 5 minutes (5 minutes is probably bit aggressive , in real production environments you may want to trigger alarms if the threshold is breached for a duration longer than 5 minutes).

4. Click on *"create Alarm"*.

We started with reactive monitoring of prebuilt metrics on AWS CloudWatch, published custom metrics to CloudWatch based on our needs .Moved to automated monitoring using triggered emails based on alarms on CloudWatch metrics.

---

[10] For more information on email triggers for alarms please refer AWS documentation *http://docs.aws.amazon.com/AmazonCloudWatch/latest/DeveloperGuide/US_AlarmAtThresh oldEC2.html*

MongoDB on AWS

Additional References

Chapter 1

- No SQL databases

  http://www.odbms.org/wp-content/uploads/2014/03/Implementing_a_NoSQL_Strategy.pdf

  https://en.wikipedia.org/wiki/NoSQL

- CAP Theorem

  http://groups.csail.mit.edu/tds/papers/Gilbert/Brewer2.pdf

Chapter 2

- Cloud computing by amazon

  https://aws.amazon.com/what-is-cloud-computing/?nc2=h_l2_cc

MongoDB on AWS

- Getting started with AWS

  https://aws.amazon.com/getting-started/?nc2=h_l2_cc

- EC2 Introduction , pricing and instances types

  http://aws.amazon.com/ec2/

  http://aws.amazon.com/ec2/instance-types/

  http://aws.amazon.com/ec2/pricing/

Chapter 3

- MongoDB on AWS , quick start reference deployment

  https://aws.amazon.com/blogs/aws/mongodb-on-the-aws-cloud-new-quick-start-reference-deployment/

- AWS Cloud formation

  http://aws.amazon.com/cloudformation/

- Sample cloud formation sample templates

  http://aws.amazon.com/cloudformation/aws-cloudformation-templates/

- VPC with public and Private Subnets

  http://docs.aws.amazon.com/AmazonVPC/latest/UserGu

Additional References

CCLX

MongoDB on AWS

ide/VPC_Scenario2.html

- o Master Slave replication in MongoDB

    http://docs.mongodb.org/manual/core/master-slave/

Chapter 4

- o MongoDB replica set deployment

    http://docs.mongodb.org/manual/tutorial/deploy-replica-set/

Chapter 5

- o MongoDB sharding introduction

    http://docs.mongodb.org/manual/core/sharding-introduction/

- o MongoDB sharding guide

    http://docs.mongodb.org/master/MongoDB-sharding-guide.pdf

Chapter 6

- o Amazon simple storage service (S3).

    http://aws.amazon.com/s3/

Additional References

CCLXI

MongoDB on AWS

o Amazon Glacier.

http://aws.amazon.com/glacier/

o RAID configuration on AWS EC2.
http://docs.aws.amazon.com/AWSEC2/latest/UserGui
de/raid-config.html

o AWS CLI commands for EBS
http://docs.aws.amazon.com/AWSEC2/latest/UserGui
de/ebs-api-cli-overview.html

Chapter 7

o MongoDB backup methods
http://docs.mongodb.org/manual/core/backups/

o Automating EBS snapshots using Python.
https://pypi.python.org/pypi/automated-ebs-snapshots

Chapter 8

o MMS
https://www.mongodb.com/cloud

o MMS alerts for MongoDB deployment

Additional References

CCLXII

MongoDB on AWS

https://www.mongodb.com/blog/post/five-mms-
monitoring-alerts-keep-your-mongodb-deployment-
track

- o Some EC2 metrics that everyone should monitor

  http://docs.aws.amazon.com/AWSEC2/latest/UserGui
  de/monitoring_ec2.html

- o Amazon CloudWatch

  http://aws.amazon.com/cloudwatch/

www.ingramcontent.com/pod-product-compliance
Lightning Source LLC
Chambersburg PA
CBHW070939050326
40689CB00014B/3267